**INSIGHT**

Goa

Compact Guide: Goa is the ultimate quick-reference guide to this lively destination. It tells you all you need to know about the attractions of Goa, not only exploring its beaches but also its rich heritage, from Buddhist caves to Hindu temples and Portuguese churches to colonial mansions.

This is one of 133 Compact Guides, combining the interests and enthusiasms of two of the world's best-known information providers: Insight Guides, whose innovative titles have set the standard for visual travel guides since 1970, and Discovery Channel, the world's premier source of nonfiction television programming.

APA PUBLICATIONS

Part of the Langenscheidt Publishing Group

Star Attractions

An instant reference to some of Goa's most popular tourist attractions to help you to set your priorities.

Panaji Church p20

Fontainhas p22

Basilica of Bom Jesus p28

Boat Tours p31

Shri Shantadurga Temple p35

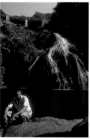

Dudhsagar Falls p38

Northern beaches p39

Mapusa's Friday Market p48

Menezes-Braganza House p56

Palolem Beach p60

Excursion to Hampi p63

Introduction

Places

Culture

Leisure

Practical Information

Goa – A Place Apart

Pleasure-seekers have lingered along Goa's golden coast-line since myth and legend gave way to written history. In the ancient Hindu epic *Mahabharata*, battle-weary Lord Parasurama longed for a peaceful spot fit for meditation and fired an arrow from the forests of the Western Ghats straight into the Arabian Sea. There, a sea god helped him to reclaim Gomant, an idyllic island between two rivers which is now part of Goa, India's 25th state.

The pace in Goa is more laid-back than almost any-where else on the sub-continent. Beachcombers and lo-cals alike take time out for a siesta after feasting on fish curry, then sip a few beers at sundown. Though Goa was a Portuguese outpost for over 400 years, don't expect an Iberian lifestyle transposed to the tropics: this is India, and stunted cattle pick their way around sunbathers and co-conut palms with impunity.

Beach scene

Portuguese seafarers, who struggled against established Muslim traders and Moghul intruders to claim Goa's strategic deep-water ports along the old spice route, were as captivated by the local Konkan beauties as by the booty they found. After Jesuit missionaries, taking over from St Francis Xavier, targeted this remote region, cruel Inquisitors hounded the local Hindus into the hinterlands. Though many venerable temples were demolished along the coast, where white village churches and wayside crosses now mark the landscape and nearly one third of the people are Catholic, Hindu festivals are still vibrant in Goa. Images once kept clandestine are venerated in glorious new temples that fuse Islamic or Portuguese baroque themes into exuberant Hindu architecture.

5

Cross in Cavelossim

Venture away from the usual beach resorts and clifftop forts, and unexpected discoveries await. Elegant colo-nial manors with carved hardwood furniture open up for lucky passers-by. Huts set in scruffy cashew groves sell freshly toasted nuts, dusted with a fiery masala on request. In some village churches, hymns are sung in lilt-ing Konkani to the accompaniment of fiddles. Ancient Buddhist rock temples and wildlife re-serves teeming with exotic birds and reptiles dot the landscape.

Location and landscape

Found midway down the western coast of India, tucked between the states of Maharashtra and Kar-nataka, tropical Goa is India's smallest state. Shaped rather like a battered lace fan, it covers just 3,700 sq km (1,420 sq miles), roughly the size of America's Rhode Island, only at 15 degrees latitude. There are six principal tidal rivers – from

Paddies near Cabo de Rama

Salt pans at Gokarn

Pineapple flower

north to south: the Tirakol, Chapora, Mandovi, Zuari, Sal and Talpona – and countless small inlets, the largest of them lined by mangroves.

Like folds of a fan, dark laterite outcrops dramatically interrupt broad beaches along most of the fabled shoreline that stretches over 105km (65 miles). Sand dunes mimic the rolling breakers with parallel sets that extend behind the widest beaches.

In the lowlands, coconut and areca nut palms are cultivated. The graceful trees mark the margins of extensive paddy fields that turn a brilliant parakeet green when the rice shoots are tender – a stark contrast to the nubbled brown fields out of season. Slow ferries ply the rivers, laden with coir cargo and commuters.

The coastal plateau extends some 30km (18 miles) inland, considerably further than in neighbouring states, and can support banana, pineapple, mango and jackfruit wherever there is sufficient topsoil. Pale vanilla orchids or spiky pepper vines are coaxed to grow beneath cashew trees, which are a major cash crop, with enough leftovers to be brewed into the potent *kaju feni* liquor which fuels virtually all the Goan fiestas, along with coconut feni, palm toddy or local port wine.

The stepped highlands of the Western Ghats, the Sahyadri range, continues for another 35km (22 miles) to the Karnataka border. At places the crests are more than 1,000m (3,300ft) high. Most dramatic of all is Dudhsagar Falls, where the Kandhepar River tumbles from a height of 600m (2,000ft) to make a frothy 'milk flow' – the literal translation of Dudhsagar. Narrow gorges lead up into the craggy highlands, where fire-resistant sal and teak trees that withstand diminishing attempts at slash and burn agriculture are plentiful. This rainforest also supplies many rare plants used in traditional Ayurvedic cures.

Open-cast manganese and iron-ore mines mar some of this interior landscape with ugly slagheaps, but are happily tolerated because of the profits the exports produce. Iron ore outstrips tourism as the state's prime foreign currency earner.

Climate

There can be a lot of microclimates within the Western Ghats, changing according to the altitude, the direction of the wind, and the drainage of the rugged landscape. But in general Goa has three basic seasons. It is splendid between November and late February, when the air temperature matches the balmy sea water and is sufficiently cooled by evening breezes that a wrap may be required at night. Things get muggy between mid-March and May, when sodden air begins to build up in pre-monsoon temperatures that hover around 33°C (90°F). It's still rather uncomfortable post-monsoon, in September and October, particularly in the foothills, when the storms let up and the steaming humidity has no release. The weather is wet and wild from mid-June to the end of August, when the sea roils with flotsam and jetsam and muddy backwash from rivers in full spate. Winds whip up and lightning crackles across the sky. Typically, 2,500mm (1,200 in) of torrential rain drenches Goa during the monsoon season, more than twice India's national average, but there are daily periods when these downpours cease and the atmosphere seems magical. High thunderclouds tend to dump their loads as soon as they hit the first barrier of the Western Ghats. Just across the border in Karnataka, the forest cover in the Ghats is drier and sparser because of this phenomenon.

Old-fashioned Portuguese arcades, which shield equally from the sun and the rain, are ideal for Goan weather and central Panaji's traditional pillared shops and offices continue this Iberian style. Similarly, the wide verandahs on traditional bungalows help to beat the heat and damp.

Colomatera arcades

7

People

Goa's population, estimated at 1.3 million, continues to be mostly rural, with only 41 percent living in town. Yet thousands more live in economic exile. A high proportion of families must cope with the absence of fathers or sons who migrate across the Arabian Gulf to work as skilled labourers, to India on cruise liners or with Portuguese passports to Britain and other EU countries. Many return briefly each spring, laden with duty-free perfume or electronic gear, anxious to make up for staying away so long. The itinerant pop musicians who play on India's five-star hotel circuit or on cruise ships are almost invariably young Goans, known for their ability to cover hit songs and stay on key. Most boast distinctive good looks with broad smiles.

Mayem Lake guide

Goa's location as a distant port with restricted access by land has resulted in unexpected combinations of colouring and features. Once outsiders strayed into this exotic outpost, they tended to stay and intermingle. Historically, the trade centre of Goa became an extraordinary melting pot. Over the years, honey-skinned Konkans resulted from Dravidian tribes mixing with Aryan settlers. Successive waves of foreigners kept coming to the well-sited ports. Mauryan soldiers called this province Aparanta or 'Beyond the End' and eventually were superceded by militant Hindu dynasties and then by rich Arab traders who imported warhorses across the Gulf for military officers, swapping steeds for silk and spices. Next came Mughal warriors, followed by Portuguese seamen, conquistadors sworn to extinguish Islam, and colonists seeking fortunes.

A smile from Calangute

Early Portuguese settlers were urged by the church to marry local women, and the resulting light eyes, wavy hair and fair skin are seen as marks of prestige in a society that still is caste-conscious. Yet it would be hard to pin-point a set of typical Goan features.

Common Portuguese surnames – such as Dias, Souza, Rodrigues or Pereira – might seem like an obvious give-away of European ancestry, but it's easy to be misled. These colonial names also were adopted – minus the noble family prefix, Da – by Khavi fishermen, direct descendants of Goa's original Dravidian inhabitants who first reclaimed coastal land from the sea by building up break-waters and sluices to form *khazans*.

Family names, as everywhere in India, often denote caste. High-born families were enticed to convert to Catholicism during the years of Portuguese rule by being allowed to keep all their traditional privileges. Even today, classified ads for arranged marriages between Goan Christians usually specify the desired caste of both bride and groom. Identity is all-important, and there is a slot for every group in the ancient hierarchy.

Sweepers and indigenous tribes rank beneath the system, but are not shunned completely. Tribal Kunbi women, goatherds with copper bangles protecting their forearms like armour and bead necklaces covering their chests, often turn up at Goan bazaars. Loin-cloth clad Gavde Adivasis, who are animistic trappers and fishermen, have not been so assimilated into town life.

A lamani trader

Religion: diversity and harmony

Most Goans are Hindu. Catholics make up 30 percent of the population, and along with nuns and priests from Kerala and Tamil Nadu, provide most of India's Christian clergy. The academic standards of private convent schools are high and Goan students of all religions vie for a chance to be taught by nuns. (The few Koranic schools are mostly restricted to followers of Islam.) Education in English is valued because it increases job opportunities abroad. Goa's literacy rate of 82 percent is considerably better than the Indian average.

Local nuns

Since so many Hindus and Christians study together, and for generations have shared the same neighbourhoods, quite a few devotional rituals appear to be odd hybrids. This is also due to the persecution of Hindus by Muslim raiders in the 14th century, followed by the suppression of Hinduism by zealous Portuguese missionaries for 210 years during the Inquisition. An early Church policy allowed new converts to worship and pray with familiar rites, so some confusion is inevitable.

Local adoration of the Virgin Mary and sundry minor saints involves flower garlands and plenty of incense, al-

most indistinguishable from the reverence shown for the female Hindu deities known as *devis*. In Mapusa, the Hindu goddess Lairaya is prayed to by devout Christians, who know her as Our Lady of Miracles. Many Catholic priests in Goa still retain their Brahmin status and beneath the cassock wear the Hindu sacred thread.

Modern Hindu temples in Goa have domed towers of painted stucco, inspired by Islamic architecture. Elaborate *tulsi* platforms for sacred basil plants resemble wayside crosses in rural Portugal, only more brightly coloured. Many details are derived from colonial Christian notions of worship. None resemble the classic Shiva temple at Tambdi Surla, near the Karnataka border, the only one left in Goa that pre-dates the Portuguese conquest.

Party-going Goans set great store by celebrating each other's religious holidays. Lord Krishna's birthday, with mass bathing off Diwadi Island in the Mandovi River, can get nearly as rowdy as the pre-Lent Carnival. So can the spring revelry of Holi – though Diwali, the Hindu festival of lights, is considerably tamer than in firecracker-mad North India. Everybody celebrates Christmas and New Year, when cheerful paper star lanterns – lucky symbols for Christians, Hindus and Muslims alike – are suspended over public thoroughfares.

Just 5 percent of Goans are Muslim, even though Islam has been practised in Goa since Arab merchants arrived from the Malabar coast in the 1st millennium AD. Many work as craftsmen and live close to the impressive Safa Masjid at Ponda, Goa's oldest mosque, or near the Jama Masjid in Panaji. Islamic women often veil themselves with voluminous black *burqas*, despite the heat, whenever they go out in public. They normally go with a bearded male escort wearing a skullcap. Others don long tunics over baggy drawstring trousers and drape a scarf over their bosom for modesty. (Some Hindu women find this *salwar*

Inside Mallikarjun Temple and Our Lady of Miracles

Diwali/Christmas lantern in Anjuna

Travellers in Gokarn

kamiz more practical to wear than the sari and their conservative families prefer it to short skirts or tight jeans.)

Buddhism, first introduced by Emperor Ashoka to the region, endured for more than 800 years in court circles, but now is negligible. Only a tiny fraction of Goans are devout Jains (0.04 percent) or Sikhs (0.02 percent).

More than four decades after independence from Portugal in 1961, with recent improvements in transport links overland, there has been an upsurge of Indian migrants from other regions. Peddlers from war-torn Kashmir, Lamani "gypsies" from Karnataka and Rajasthan who hawk fruit and trinkets, Tibetan refugees who sell *thankas* and silver charms, plus indigent road labourers from Bihar and interior Maharashtra can be seen now. There is some friction with established locals, who don't always share the same work ethic as these newcomers. The new arrivals also get the blame for any communal tensions that might crop up between Hindus, Muslims, and Christians. Indigenous Goans are proud of their reputation for religious tolerance.

Western veneer

Tourism

Until the completion of the Konkan Railway in 1999, it took longer to reach Goa overland from Bombay, the nearest big city, than by charter flight from Europe. Cut off from neighbouring states, Goa retained its distinctive lifestyle linked to rhythms of the sea and the soil. Alternative travellers in the late 1960s considered it a haven and spread its legend anew. Goa now welcomes at least 80,000 British tourists each winter, including increasing numbers of package-tour visitors and gap-year travellers: this is more than all the British inhabitants of India at the height of the Raj. Israeli and Japanese backpackers add variety to the international mix of visitors from Australia, Europe and North America. Lately, middle-class sybarites from Bombay and Delhi have started to buy second homes or condominiums in Goa, and their trendy parties give a lift to an already animated Christmas–New Year season.

Now that the Konkan railway has cut down the time it takes to complete the gruelling journey cross-country by one-third, Goa is just a 30-hour trip away from Delhi. Pessimists predict that visitors may soon outnumber Goan residents during high season. Plans for a second international airport, at Mopa in Pernem, have yet to be approved but alarm the anti-growth lobbyists.

Tranquil spots are still plentiful away from the popular beach resorts, where all but 5 percent of foreign tourists congregate. Melancholy *mando* love songs have not completely succumbed to the thump of techno-rave everywhere. Hustle and hassle are still comparatively rare in spite of so many rapid changes.

Peaceful Palolem Beach

Administration and politics

Goa's geography divides the state naturally into just two zones, which break up into 11 smaller divisions known as *talukas*. The north, around the capital Panaji, includes the *talukas* Tiswadi, Bardez, Bicholim, Pernem, Ponda and Satari. The south, with Margao as the commercial centre, comprises Mormugao, Salcete, Sanguem, Quepem and Canacona.

Local democracy at work

On a grassroots level, the Panchayat system works very democratically. Elected officials dispense justice locally like the village elders used to do. But the state government, made up of 40 legislative assembly members, has witnessed considerable turmoil in recent years. Successive fractious coalition governments in Delhi have made canny alliances hard to predict. Goa was put under direct rule from Delhi after practically going bankrupt in 1999 – a state of affairs that was blamed on corruption. In 2002 Manohar Parrikar became Goa's chief minister. Like many previous governments in Goa, this was seen as a fragile coalition cobbled together after frantic political manoeuvering. In the past 15 years, Goa has seen 14 governments. The BJP is the single largest party, with 17 seats out of the 40 Goa assembly seats. In early 2005 the Parrikar-led BJP coalition was dismissed by the State Governor and a Congress-led state government, under Paratap Singh Rane (who became Goa's 18th chief minister), was installed in its place. This move provoked howls of outrage from the BJP opposition in Delhi and the controversy looks certain to continue.

11

Home with the catch

New environmentalist parties are backed by the local Church and are gaining increased support. Regional policies in Goa are distinct from those of its big neighbour, Maharashtra, which has a Hindu nationalist majority. By committing itself to the Konkani language in the 1980s, Goa asserted its independence from Maharashtra, which had considered the local language to be a mere dialect. It was recognised as an official Indian language in 1992.

Economy and industry

Goa is relatively prosperous by Indian standards, despite its small size. More than 40,000 traditional fishermen haul in catches of shrimp and sardines daily, and continue to harvest mussels and crabs as well as game fish. Families managed to live off the sea for many generations, even though the monsoons cut the season short. Recent overfishing by off-shore trawlers is ringing alarm bells in the industry, and new commercial shrimp and fish farms have added to the controversy by introducing ecological hazards. Many fishermen can earn more by moonlighting as tourist guides, hiring their boats to day-trippers or even leasing their own homes to long-stay visitors for months at a time.

Cashew flowers

Among the plantations at Galjibag

Mining legacy (above) and Cabo de Rama vegetation

Manufacturers produce fertiliser, textiles, pharmaceuticals, iron pellets, sugar and chemicals. Rice is grown extensively, often yielding two crops a year. Exports include coconuts and coir products such as mattresses, matting and rope, plus cashew nuts, betel nuts, table salt, tropical fruit, peppercorns, cinnamon quills and medicinal herbs. Bauxite, manganese and iron ore are also important exports. Land speculation is on the increase, though waste disposal, sewage treatment and sufficient water supply are all paramount concerns if unregulated development is allowed to persist.

Environment

Environmental activists in Goa tend to concentrate on preserving traditional village life. Once mocked for wanting to keep Goa backward, and content to recycle waste via primitive 'pig toilets' – dry outhouses built above pits where hungry sows grunt expectantly as villagers defecate – these green politicians are no longer dismissed as cranks.

Water scarcity continues to be the most basic concern in a coastal society which must reclaim plots of land from the sea in order to grow sufficient food for a population that includes immigrants and seasonal tourists. If the water table is allowed to drop, many wells become saline and unusable. By late February, significant numbers of village wells dry up completely.

To prevent valuable rainwater from washing directly into the sea, numerous government dams were approved in the 1970s. Environmentalists point to these schemes, particularly the Sealulim Dam in south Goa, as tragically short-sighted. Costs soared after delays due to political scandals, and the benefactors of the diverted water proved to be a tourist resort and a chemical plant rather than coastal farmers. Removing hill tribes from their ancestral land to a substitute site, then clear-cutting the wooded slopes only increased soil erosion. What's more, 700 treeless hectares (1,800 acres) affected the water cycle adversely and annual rainfall ultimately decreased.

Activists opposed the Konkan railway, with its 92 tunnels blasted through the Western Ghats and fragile ecosystems nearby, for similar ill effects. Luxury resorts and condominiums, complete with golf courses, swimming pools and manicured lawns, are viewed as ecologically incorrect.

Opencast mines exacerbate soil erosion exponentially, and run-off silt from iron-ore mining sites can make adjacent paddyfields lie fallow for years. A programme to mass-plant cashew saplings in the hope of preventing the slagheaps from ruining agricultural land is underway, and chemical industries on the coast are being pressured to curb toxic wastes from fertiliser processing.

Wildlife

Nature lovers will find a visit to one of the wildlife sanctuaries well worthwhile. Flocks of parakeets wheel in the sky above the Western Ghat rainforests, where flying squirrels leap between vine-draped branches that support more than 80 varieties of orchid. Jungle cats and civets stalk the shadows. Big mammals to watch out for at Bhagwan Mahaveer Sanctuary, Goa's largest park, include gaur bison, spotted deer and sambar stags. Panthers – a recent census counted 18 in this reserve – may well be tracking these same species as prey, though white-faced langurs and macaques are apt to raise a shrill warning. Hyenas won't be far behind. Cotigao, in the south, is only a third as big, and it takes patience to see more than just deer and monkeys. Listen out for the barking deer.

Keep alert and you can find almost as much fauna outside the game parks. Both the mugger and the rarer saltwater crocodile, which grows three times as big, lurk in quiet estuaries and creeks. Also look out for the endangered olive Ridley sea turtles as they emerge to lay their eggs on select Morgim and Craljibag beaches. They are not nearly as common as the black-pond and flap-shell freshwater varieties. Dolphins can be spotted in the sea off most of the resorts.

Reptiles range in size from house geckoes to monitor lizards and are plentiful everywhere. Also common are fruit bats and the slightly bigger 'flying foxes' hanging upside down in the treetops. If a lone creature swoops by on silent wings after dusk, it's probably an owl rather than a bat.

Brilliant-plumed kingfishers perch on telephone wires and branches, and keen ornithologists can also tick off paradise fly-catchers, hoopoes, hornbills, egrets, eagles, seagulls, cormorants, storks, and many more. Dr Salim Ali Bird Sanctuary, on Chorao Island northeast of Panaji, is probably the best spot for serious birdwatching.

Warden's warning

Crocodiles at Bondla

Driving home the conservation message

Historical Highlights

c100,000BC Stone Age tools on upper stretches of Krishna River, just inland from Goa, are dropped by aboriginal migrants from Africa.

c2000BC Settled agriculture reaches India's west coast.

c600BC By now, Indo-Aryan settlers mix with Dravidian forest tribes. Sanskrit epics are composed, with the myth of Gomant reclaimed from the sea as their origin.

c250BC Aparanta, the province 'Beyond the End', is colonised by Ashoka, the 2nd Mauryan Emperor. Puna, his official missionary, preaches Buddhism to Goan animists.

232BC Hindu Bhoja dynasty rules from Chandrapur (now Chandor), launching seven centuries of Hindu supremacy.

AD100–300 Arab traders cross the Gulf, drawn by Indian gems, spices, and silks.

600–800 Chalukyas become the suzerains of the Goan coast from their Deccan stronghold.

1052 The Kadambas found a capital at the Zuari river port, Govapuri (Gopakaputtana). Traders call it Gove, and send ships from the Malabar Coast, Sri Lanka, Nicobar and East Africa.

1307–25 Tales of wealth in Sandapur (an Arab name for Goa) reach Delhi. Sultan Ala ud Din Khalji and his son, Muhammed Tughlaq, raid temple treasures and carry off more than 1,000 camel-loads of loot from southern and west-coast outposts, maybe as far as Goa.

1350–88 Goa's Hindu dynasty is driven out by the Bahmanis, Muslim invaders from the north. Idols and temples are hidden away after priests are brutally murdered.

1378 The Vijayanagar Empire (ruled by the King of Hampi) massacres Muslims in Goa.

1471 Bahmani leader Muhammed Shah II launches assaults on the Vijayanagar occupying forces. Bahmanis found a new capital, Ela, after destroying Goa Velha (Old Goa/Govepuri).

1490 Sultanate of Bijapur set up by Bahmani heir, Yusuf Adil Shah. He builds a fort and mosque at Mandovi, and a lavish summer palace at Panaji for his harem.

1498 Vasco da Gama lands his caravel on the Malabar coast, proving that Asia can be reached by sailing round the Cape of Good Hope.

1500 Pedro Alvares Cabral lands briefly at Goa on his return journey from the 'discovery' of Brazil.

1506 Treaty of Tordesillas. Pope Alexander's decision to use the 48th longitude as a dividing line effectively hands Asia, Africa and Brazil to Portugal and the rest of the New World to Spain.

1510 Alfonso de Albuquerque takes on Muslim pirates after Vijayanagar's Captain Timoja tells him of their whereabouts. At Panjim (Panaji), Portuguese forces triumph without a shot. Ismail Adil Khan, the teenage Bijapur Sultan, sets a three-month siege against the Portuguese, but Albuquerque wins a victory on St Catherine's Day (25 November). His alliance with the Vijayanagar ensures Hindu safety in Portuguese Goa.

1541 Portuguese conquerors order the closure of Hindu temples. Iberian traders establish a monopoly on cotton textiles for Southeast Asia and increase profits on pearls and spices.

1542 St Francis Xavier, a Jesuit priest, arrives in Goa to teach at a seminary. He goes on to win 30,000 converts in India, Malacca, and Japan.

1545 King Dom Joao II sends in more Jesuit priests. Collective worship by Hindus is banned and more than 350 shrines are looted for idols.

1560 The Inquisition begins in Goa and suspected heretics are tortured on St Catherine's wheels, with thumbscrews, or with burning candles and sulphur. *Autos-da-fé* are organised for the masses. Hindu icons are hidden in jungle sanctuaries while Inquisitors set up headquarters in Adil Shah's summer palace at Panjim.

1565 After the Vijayanagar Empire's defeat at Battle of Talikota, Muslim Sultans gain power in the south and sack Hampi.

1570 Ten-month siege by a Muslim alliance, led by the Bijapur Sultans, punishes the Portuguese for their loyalty to the Vijayanagar Empire.

1571 Bahmanis grant all rights over Old Conquests to the Portuguese.

1600–34 Goa's population swells to 225,000, comparable to Lisbon or Antwerp, though the headcount is boosted by thousands of slaves.

1603 Dutch ships blockade Goa, in an attempt to break Portugal's cotton textile monopoly.

1616 Jesuit translators render the New Testament as a Konkani folktale that will appeal to Konkan villagers.

1635 Epidemics of typhoid, cholera and malaria sweep through Goa's port cities. Portuguese convicts are brought in to boost numbers after a rapid decline in the population. The Convention of Goa allows the British East India Company to trade freely in Portuguese holdings.

1639 Dutch frigates blockade Goa again. Protestant traders try to muscle in on lucrative Eastern routes, with notable successes in Malacca by 1641, Cochin in 1657 and Ceylon in 1663.

1667–83 Maratha troops, led by Shivaji, gain control of surrounding regions. His son, Sambhaji, siezes a trading post at Chaul. A Portuguese incursion against Ponda fails. St Francis Xavier's coffin is opened and Portuguese leaders pray for the saint's divine intercession. The Marathas retreat from Old Goa to fight the Moghuls.

1737–9 Marathas seize Bardez and Salcete, but withdraw in exchange for the Portuguese-held Bassein, near Bombay. A truce is signed in May 1739, and the Portuguese claim victory.

1780–2 Bicholim and Satari, rural districts west of Mapsa, are ceded to Portugal, as the first of the Novas Conquistas, or 'New Conquests'. To celebrate, Goans demand an open display of St Francis Xavier's relics in the Basilica of Bom Jesus, sparking a fervent religious reaction.

1787 The Pinto Revolt, a failed plot in Candolim to overthrow the ruling government, results in the public execution of 15 priests in Panjim.

1791 The Rajah of Sunda gives up Ponda, Sanguem, Canacona and Quepem to the Portuguese, putting all Goa under Iberian rule.

1799–1813 British troops occupy Fort Aguada in a bid against French forces, allied with Tipu Sultan of Mysore, during the Napoleonic wars.

1812 The Inquisition finally ceases in Goa, 38 years after official orders from Lisbon to stop.

1821 Goa sends representatives to the parliament in Lisbon for the first time.

1839 A British offer to buy Goa for £500,000 sterling is rejected by Lisbon.

1843 Viceroy Dom Manuel de Portugal e Castro declares Panjim the capital of Goa.

1881 A railway line finally joins Mormagao to the rest of India.

1905 Manganese and iron-ore mines open.

1928 Goa Congress Party founded.

1946 Leaders of Azad Gomank Dal, militants for Goan independence, are deported to Lisbon.

1947 India becomes independent.

1955 Civil disobedience tactics by Goan nationalists countered by 4,000 Portuguese troops.

1961 After 451 years of Portuguese occupation, Prime Minister Jawaharlal Nehru summons the Indian Army and liberates Goa.

1987 Goa becomes India's 25th state on 30 May. A 'master plan' seeks big-spending tourists.

1992 Konkani is recognised as the 18th official Indian language.

2000 Konkani adopted as the state language.

2004 St Francis Xavier's body is displayed for Panaji's decennial "Exposition" and the capital hosts an International Film Festival.

2005 Congress politician Paratap Singh Rane becomes chief minister.

Church of Our Lady of the Immaculate Conception
Preceding pages: Baga Beach

Route 1

Panaji/Panjim and environs

Praça de Flores – Idalcan's Palace – Statue of Abbe Faria – Institute Menezes Braganza and Library – Azad Maidan – Mahalakshmi Temple – Altinho Hill – Fontainhas – State Archeological Museum – Sao Tome – Campal – Miramar Beach – Dona Paula – Cabo Raj Bhavan (14km/9 miles) *See map opposite*

Downtown Panaji

Overlooking the mouth of the Mandovi River, 10 km (6 miles) upstream from the former colonial city, Panaji (most commonly referred to by its local name, Panjim) is Goa's bustling capital. With a population nudging 100,000, the town forms a hub for domestic tourists from other Indian states, who stay in its many modern hotels and guests houses. Foreign visitors, on the other hand, tend to come here on day trips to shop and wander around the atmospheric old colonial quarter, still holding its own against the phalanx of apartment blocks that now crowd the outskirts. Most of this tour's sights are within walking distance and there are plenty of good restaurants and places to stay.

History

Originally, **Panaji** was a little fishing village near the mouth of the **Mandovi River**. It was first mentioned on an inscribed copper plate from the Kadamba Era around 1100 as the village of Pahajan/Pahajanikali or 'land that does not flood', since it was surrounded by swamps. Some historians believe that it was derived from an Urdu name meaning five enchanted castles, since there were five Muslim forts on hilltops around here during the 14th century.

The strategic location of the site was first recognised by the Bijapuri Sultan Yusuf Adil Shah and he built a magnificent fortress-palace on the waterfront in 1500. However, Alfonso de Albuquerque eventually took the fort and rebuilt it. Later, it became a custom-clearing point for ships approaching the old city of Goa downstream and a military outpost. A chapel was erected in 1541 on the site of the present Church of Our Lady of the Immaculate Conception so that the disembarking Portuguese sailors could offer thanksgiving for their safe voyage. Gradually, after some land-reclamation, the viceroy at the time had a 3-km (1¾-mile) causeway built over the marshland between Panjim (as it was known) and Old Goa, now known as the Ribander Causeway (formerly Ponte de Linhares).

New arrivals

Old Goa was abandoned by the Portuguese in the 18th century following a spate of epidemics and the viceroy eventually took up residence at the old Bijapuri palace. Soon followed by Portuguese nobility who reclaimed more land in order to build their homes here, Panjim became the capital of choice instead of Mormugao. In the 19th century the governor, Dom Manuel Portíe Castro, developed the town further by reclaiming more land, constructing roads, municipal buildings and institutions. The city was renamed Nova Goa, and in 1843 was officially recognised as the capital of Portugal's most remote colony in Asia.

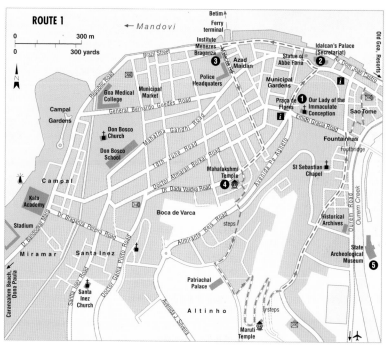

School's out on Church Square

After Goa gained its independence from Portugal in 1961 and became an Indian State in 1987, Panjim retained its status as the capital, but was re-named Panaji. The enormous new Vidhan Sabha (State Government Headquarters) occupies a prime spot on a hill at Porvorim across the Mandovi Bridge facing Panaji. A similarly expensive project was the massive facelift the town received ahead of the 2004 International Film Festival, when the waterfront promenade was enlarged and approach roads re-surfaced.

Sights

This tour starts near the tree-shaded Municipal Gardens edged with a variety of shops and restaurants near the Main Square or **Praça de Flores** (Square of Flowers), dominated by the whitewashed baroque facade of the church of ★★ **Our Lady of the Immaculate Conception ❶**. Originally built in 1541 for Portuguese sailors, new architectural features were added over the years, including the unusual processional stairway. The present building was erected in 1619 and modelled on the church at Reis Magos. High-vaulted ceilings and beautiful gilded reredos behind the altars and marble statues of the two apostles, St Peter and St Paul, mark the interior, while the central belfry outside houses the second largest bell in Goa. There is a statue of **Our Lady of Fatima**, wearing a crown of gold and diamonds, that was installed here in 1945. On 13 October each year, it is carried in a candlelight procession.

Idalcan's Palace

North of the square, take the road to the Secretariat on the banks of the Mandovi river. This former palace of Adil Shah of Bijapur was converted to a trading post and temporary residence for viceroys by the Portuguese who called it **Idalcan's Palace ❷**. Possibly the oldest building in town, with a sloping red-tiled roof and wooden verandahs facing the waterfront, the main entrance is a Romanesque arch which once had the viceroy's crest, now replaced by India's Ashoka Chakra (King Ashoka's wheel of law) since it used to house the state legislature.

Abbe Faria and patient

On the west side of the main promenade (Avenida Dom Joao Castro/D. Bandodkar Marg) is a strange, but striking ★ **statue** depicting the figure of a man leaning over an unconscious woman who is actually supposed to be in a hypnotic trance. The man is **Abbé Faria**, born in 1755 in Goa and of mixed Portuguese/Goan heritage. Today he is considered a pioneer in hypnosis, although at the time he was publicly denounced by the Church due to the scandal caused by his hypnotic seances. He wrote a defence *On the Cause of Lucid Sleep*, which was published in 1819 shortly before his death.

Continue on the promenade past the State Bank on the left and turn left onto Malacca Road which leads to the ★★ **Institute Menezes Braganza ❸** and the Central

Library, housed in a wing of an old military building complex. This scientific and literary institution was founded in 1871 as the Institute Vasco da Gama (on the anniversary of the day he rounded the Cape of Good Hope) and later renamed after a hero of the Goan Independence movement – a journalist from a prominent family, Luis Menezes de Braganza (1878–1938). At present it has 24 fellows, who are all distinguished Goan citizens.

The entrance hall displays four detailed murals depicting scenes from the epic poem, *Os Lusiadas*, by the Portuguese poet Luis Vaz de Camoes, a critic of colonialism. The ★ **murals** are made with *azulejos* (blue painted tiles on a yellow background) and illustrate the Portuguese exploration of South Asia. Starting from the one to the left of the entrance, each picture has a verse from the poem as well. All are in sequence. Through a door here is the oldest public **library** in India, etablished in 1832 (Monday to Friday, 9.30am–1.15pm and 2–5.45pm). It has a rich collection of old texts, manuscripts and religious treasures from the churches of Old Goa.

Upstairs, the small ★ **Antonio de Doronho Art Gallery** (same opening times) displays prints and paintings by local artists, as well as secondhand books and maps. Before leaving the premises, stock up on some home-made Goan-style snacks, pickles or spices from the sales-counter.

Outside, walk past **Azad Maidan** marked by a pavilion built for a brass statue of Alfonso de Albuquerque which now serves as a memorial to the Goan freedom fighter Dr Tristan de Braganza Cunha, and return to the Municipal Gardens area for a break.

From the gardens, head south to visit the colourful ★ **Mahalakshmi Temple** ❹. The first Hindu temple to be permitted in Goa after the Inquisition, it was built in 1818 and was given its present form in 1983. Behind it,

Colonial mansion on Altinho Hill

21

Azad Maidan (above) and Mahalakshmi Temple

Patriarchal Palace

12th-century Ponda carving

In the Sao Tome neighbourhood

a flight of stone steps ascends **Altinho Hill** where there are several grand, but crumbling colonial mansions. It's a pleasant walk up and besides the splendid views from the top, Altinho Hill is also the site of the **Patriarchal Palace**, the residence of the Archbishop of Goa where the Pope stayed during his visit in 1989.

At the foot of the hill lies ★★ **Fontainhas**, Panaji's most interesting colonial district. The small white chapel of **St Sebastian** built around 1880 has a square in front that hosts the lively annual *festa* in mid November. The crucifix inside depicts Christ with open eyes and once hung at the Palace of the Inquisition in Old Goa, perhaps to signify His awareness of the ghastly proceedings. Cobbled squares, narrow lanes, red-tiled roofs, shuttered windows, iron balustrades and villas painted in pastel shades of blue, green and ochre, all make this area quite attractive. Look for old shops with Portuguese names, cafés and bars where the locals like to hang out. Up an alley beside the Chapel of St Sebastian, you can watch artisans painting traditional azulegos for sale in the showroom next to the Rangim Inn.

Cross the Orlem Creek on foot over an old bridge to the ★ **State Archeological Museum** ❺ (Monday to Friday 9.30am–1.15pm and 2–5.30pm), which stands in its own complex. Inside, there are pre-colonial artefacts, village deities, Sati and Hero stones and fine Jain bronzes. The Western Art Section contains Christian icons and some antique furniture, including a massive carved wooden table used by Old Goa's 17th-century Inquisitors. There is a series of photographs taken by a colonial official which includes a good portrait of the Rajput rebel leader, Dada Rane, and his heavily armed band of freedom fighters.

Cross back over the bridge and continue north into ★ **Sao Tomé**, a neighbourhood which livens up in the evenings. Go past the General Post Office that was once a tobacco trading house. The square outside was the site of public **executions** until 1843 and the mansion next door was once the **Mint**. If you're ready for a pit stop, try the Hotel Vihar, one of Panjim's best South Indian-style cafés, which stands a little further along Avenue Dom Jao Castro, or backtrack to the excellent restaurant Via Goa! which specialises in traditional Goan seafood.

The best way to see the remaining sights – Miramar Beach and Dona Paula – is to hire a taxi and head south along the main promenade, Avenue Dom Jao Castro/ D Bamdodkar Marg. This goes past the colonial suburb of **Campal**, where the Kala Academy – a frequent venue for classical Indian dance and music recitals – is located.

Miramar Beach

Continue south for 3km (1¾ miles) to **Miramar**, the nearest beach. The dark sands stretch invitingly for at least 2km (1¼ miles). This spot is good for sunset views, or a seafood meal at the popular Martin's Beach Corner restaurant at the adjoining **Caranzalem Beach**. Among its clients have been movie stars Roger Moore and Gregory Peck, who filmed *The Sea Wolves* nearby. This was once the site of a fort at Gaspar Dias, built to defend the mouth of the Mandovi, although a savage massacre left no ruins to mark the spot.

23

After 4km (2½ miles) southwest, the rocky headland of ★★ **Dona Paula** rises between the Mandovi and Zuari estuaries. Legends abound about Dona Paula, said to be a viceroy's daughter who leapt to her death from these cliffs when denied permission to marry her Goan lover. Others claim she was the governor's mistress who was punished by his wife and flung off the cliffs wearing only a string of pearls that had been his gift. In any case, Dona Paula was a wealthy Portuguese woman who donated the land around this village to her church and her tombstone is in the chapel at **Cabo Raj Bhavan**.

Dona Paula

These days, the area has been developed into up-market tourist resorts with private beaches in the little bays. The old fishing **jetty** is also the ferry point for an diverting foray (45 minutes; four times a day) across the bay to Mormugao Harbour *(see Route 8, page 53).*

Cabo Raj Bhavan has a spectacular location at the tip of a rocky promontory that extends 600m (2,000ft) from the mainland between the two rivers. Originally a chapel was built here in 1540, followed by a fort and a convent. The buildings served as a temporary residence for the archbishop from around 1650 to 1798 when it was occupied by British troops until 1813 (there is a British cemetery here, in a walled compound just below the road). Thereafter, the archbishop resided here until the viceroy took over in 1866. Since independence it has remained the residence of the governor of Goa and is therefore closed to visitors.

Sé Cathedral in Old Goa

Route 2

Old Goa

Old Goa (Sé Cathedral and Basilica of Bom Jesus) – Carambolim Lake – Pilar Seminary – Talaulim (Santanna) – Chorao Island (Dr Salim Ali Bird Sanctuary) – Divar Island – Bambolim and Siridao beaches (35km/ 19 miles) *See map on pages 26–7*

This tour visits Old Goa via a scenic route along the Mandovi River, past Chorao Island. Ribander is a ferry crossing point for Chorao Island and the place to hire boats for a trip around the bird sanctuary. A visit to Divar Island can be made by ferry from Old Goa. The tour continues south to Carambolim Lake, then Pilar Seminary. It passes the peaceful beaches at Siridao and Bambolim before returning to Panjim.

History

Deities for sale

The area around the present site of **Old Goa** was once a village of Hindu Brahmins known as Brahmapuri in the12th century. It grew into a township called Ela under the Vijayanagar kings and later became the second capital of the Bijapuri ruler, Adil Shah. After his magnificent palace here was demolished, the town grew into a major trading and ship-building centre.

In 1510, Alfonso de Albuquerque defeated the Muslims, forcibly occupied the town and soon the Portuguese had established the new colonial capital of 'Goa Dourada' (Golden Goa). When it was at its peak, the city was nicknamed 'Rome of the Orient', because of its numerous majestic baroque churches, monasteries, convents and chapels surrounded by stately homes. It had a population

larger than most of its counterparts in Europe – Lisbon, Paris or London. This magnificent city was abandoned following a spate of virulent plagues and a gradual silting of the River Mandovi. By 1835 the new capital of Nova Goa was established in Panjim, as it was known.

Today, very little remains of the town, except the religious buildings which are now a World Heritage site with some exceptional churches, including the largest church in Asia – the Sé Cathedral. These days, the gigantic facades of some of the churches rise out of the surrounding jungle where the grand villas of Goa Dourada once stood. The Archeological Survey of India maintains the grounds with their lawns and a sprinkling of benches under shady trees.

Goa's most famous Christian pilgrimage site is the Basilica of Bom Jesus which houses the incorruptible mortal remains of St Francis Xavier, patron saint of Goa. This Spanish nobleman and scholar was deeply influenced by the Jesuit leader, Ignatius Loyola. In May 1542 he arrived in Goa to preach. His stay was brief. As a missionary, he travelled to Ceylon, Malacca and Japan, then died on the island of Sancian off the Chinese coast on 2 December 1552. His body was returned to Goa when it was found to be in perfect condition months after his death. A medical examination was conducted by the viceroy's physician in 1556, but the report was acknowledged only in 1662 when he was canonised by Rome.

Bom Jesus procession

25

His holy relics were displayed each year on the anniversary of his death and thereafter, since 1859, an exposition is held every 10 or 12 years. The remains are taken to the Sé Cathedral so that the thousands of pilgrims who gather here may have easier access. The last exposition was held between November 2004 and January 2005 and was attended by an estimated 2.5 million pilgrims. The next one is scheduled for January 2014–5.

The relics were placed in a crystal urn in a silver casket in 1953 in an effort to protect them from damage. Some body parts – a toe and an arm – had been snatched away by relic enthusiasts who coveted potent holy souvenirs.

Sights

The traditional entrance to Old Goa was approached by sea from the northeastern corner of the main square. VIP visitors came through the **Viceregal Arch** – a memorial gate made of red and green granite to honour the Portuguese explorer, Vasco da Gama, in 1599. The new viceroy would pick up his set of golden keys to the city and lead other important dignitaries down the main street past traders vending the wealth of the subcontinent.

Through the arch, the first building on the path to the left is the domed, baroque Church and Convent of **St Cajetan/Caetano**. This was built by Italian friars around

Viceregal Arch

1661 and said to be modelled on St Peter's in Rome, although the cupolas have been replaced by side towers. The enormous vaulted ceiling inside has a floral motif. Statues of the apostles skilfully carved from granite stand in niches along the doorways. The main altar and the six other altars are all elaborately decorated with golden angels, cherubs and scrolls. The friars as well as some Portuguese officials were buried in a crypt below the main altar, but the last of these was finally removed to Lisbon in 1992. There are some Italian-style paintings with scenes from the life of St Cajetan and St Agnes. Beneath a net cover and an iron plaque at an altar in the centre of the church is an old well, more than 22m (72ft) deep; its water is regarded as holy.

Pilgrims in town

Nearby is a **ruined carved doorway** on a stepped platform that was once part of **Adil Shah's** wonderful palace and its lone surviving monument. The building later housed the Inquisition.

North of the main square stands the largest church in Asia, ★★ **Sé Cathedral**. Dedicated to St Catherine, this

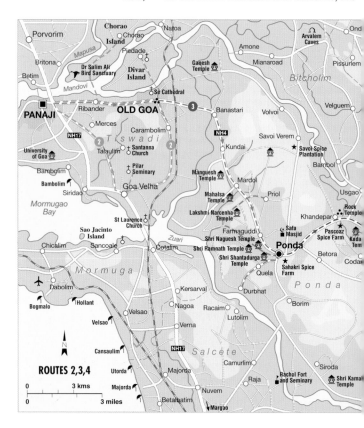

imposing church has a plain exterior that belies the immense vaulted interior with 15 altars and eight chapels. The beautifully decorated **Chapel of the Blessed Sacrament** has a gilded wooden screen and the **Cross of Miracles**, said to have increased in size miraculously since it was found by a local shepherd around 1619.

At the entrance is a huge painting of St Christopher that hangs beneath the choir, while inside the towering gilded reredos behind the main altar depict scenes from the life of St Catherine of Alexandria. An 18th-century organ is mounted on a projecting gallery in the nave and in the sacristy there is an altar with a model of St Peter's in Rome. The cathedral is also famous for housing the largest bell in Asia – known as the **Golden Bell** for its rich, mellow tone. It hangs in a towering belfry to the south of the facade. Even today, the cathedral continues to function as a parish church with its own priest.

To the east of the chapel is the lovely church and convent of ★★ **St Francis of Assisi** (1661) which was once a pre-eminent centre of the Franciscan order. Its facade

Se Cathedral facade

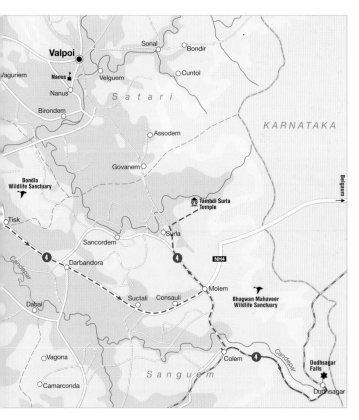

Church of St Francis of Assisi

has a niche with a granite statue of the Archangel Michael. Notable for its ornate Manueline doorway, a remnant of a former structure, it has a central nave with three chapels on each side and a main altar with a large statue of St Francis and a cross. The interior walls are covered with exquisite **frescoes** in pastel shades and gold.

The gilded reredos on the east wall features St Francis with Jesus, below whom are depicted the vows of the Franciscan Order – Poverty, Humility and Obedience. There are two side altars dedicated to St Anthony and the crucified Jesus and a small chapel to Our Lady of the Immaculate Conception.

Adjacent to the church, in an old wing of the convent, is a small ★ **Archeological Museum** (10am– 5pm; closed Friday) with a modest collection of 12th- and 13th-century sculpture, coins and manuscripts, suttee stones (in memory of widows who chose to commit suicide on their husbands' funeral pyres) and hero stones (marking the death of a warrior) as well as an interesting portrait gallery of Portuguese viceroys and governors in Goa. Close by, the small **Chapel of St Catherine**, now surrounded by greenery,was built on the spot where Albuquerque first entered the city on St Catherine's Day. Its facade with twin towers was the prototype for Se Cathedral and the churches of Goa.

To the south stands the most famous site of Christian pilgrimage in Goa – the ★★ **Basilica of Bom Jesus**, built in 1605 and dedicated to the 'infant or good Jesus'. The ornate facade is a mix of red laterite and granite. The carved basalt pillars were specially brought from Bassein, 300km (180 miles) away. The building rises in three high stages: on the ground level, the three entrances are flanked by Ionic columns; in the middle there are three windows

Altar in the Basilica of Bom Jesus

with Doric columns; and the top has circular windows between Corinthian columns. The centrepiece of the facade is the monogram 'I.H.S' – the symbol for Jesus in Greek, surrounded by wistful angels.

At the entrance and beneath the choir is the altar of St Anthony and beside it is a well-carved wooden statue of St Francis Xavier. Inside, gigantic ornate gilded reredos behind the main altar depict St Ignatius Loyala, founder of the Jesuits, and the Christ child. Above the long wooden altar there is a tall statue of the saint looking upwards at the symbol of Christ surmounted by the Holy Trinity and a host of angels.

To the right of the altar is the highlight of this church, a three-tiered ★★★ **catafalque** of Italian jasper and marble, which was presented by the Duke of Tuscany in 1698, topped by a locally made silver casket beneath which are housed the mortal remains of St Francis Xavier, missionary and saint (*see page 25*). Four bronze panels set in the base depict scenes from his life. A corridor leads to the sacristy, which has an impressively carved entrance door.

To the west, on ★★ **Holy Hill** (Monte Santo), are some of Old Goa's oldest buildings. To get there, take a brisk walk along the lane leading uphill from the bus stand. It leads past the 17th-century Church and Convent of St John of God – at present run as a home for the elderly and infirm by Hospitaller nuns.

With its unusual flying buttresses, the three-storeyed **Convent of St Monica** opposite was once the only nunnery in Goa and the first in India. It is still occupied by some cloistered sisters (whose photos appear earlier). The adjoining church is dedicated to St Monica, the mother of St Augustine, and is said to have a miraculous crucifix. It has a fine pulpit and some blue-painted *azulejo* tiles near the altar. Nearby, a ruined belfry is all that remains of the **Augustine Monastery** that once stood here and was considered the grandest building in Goa. Further uphill is the charming and evocative **Chapel of St Anthony**, one of the three churches built on the orders of Portugal's Alfonso de Albuquerque to celebrate his victory in 1510.

Augustine Monastery remains

West of St Monica's stands the oldest remaining church in Goa, built in order to fulfil a vow made on this spot by Albuquerque. The present building of this **Church of Our Lady of the Rosary** was completed in 1549. Rarely unlocked, the interior is simple and contains the marble tomb of Caterina a Piro, remembered as the first European woman to arrive at the colony. She is rumoured to have had a scandalous romance with a Portuguese nobleman, Garcia de Sa, who later became viceroy of Goa. They were eventually married at her deathbed at the behest of St Francis Xavier, who once preached here. A plaque on

Our Lady of the Rosary

the west wall records this to be the spot from which Adil Shah's army launched a counter attack on the city in 1510.

Another fine viewpoint, especially at sunset, is the top of a hill to the east of Old Goa. From the main roundabout, just east of the Basilica, take the road northwards towards the river, and then the first lane on the right to the **Church of Our Lady of the Mount**, another of the three churches founded by Albuquerque to celebrate his victory. There is a **tombstone** here with a **skull and crossbones** motif which marks the grave of the Portuguese architect Antonio Alvares Pereira, who designed the original church.

Return to the roundabout and head south towards Goa Velha. About 2km (1 mile) along the road is **Carambolim Lake**. This shallow expanse between the Mandovi and Zuari estuaries is home to several species of exotic migratory birds. The area is remarkable for being mosquito-free on account of a special algae that grows here in abundance.

Sausages for sale at Goa Velha

At **Pilar**, just to the north of Goa Velha, Capuchin monks built a church and convent on a hilltop around 1613. This complex now houses the Missionary Society of St Francis Xavier, which trains missionaries for service all over South Asia. It has a small museum (daily 10am–5pm) with some Christian relics and profuse carvings found on the site, which was formerly a Shiva temple. There are lovely stained-glass windows in the chapel and fine views from the roof of the seminary.

Church of Santanna, Talaulim

Talaulim (4km/2½ miles north of Goa Velha) is known for its Church of St Anna or ★ **Santanna** (the mother of the Virgin Mary), near the banks of the River Siridado. It has an impressive baroque facade rising in five stages with a statue of the saint in the centre, over a high-vaulted interior. An unusual statue of the saint as an old woman wearing a hat and holding a stick is a reminder of how she appeared in a vision to villagers during the 16th century.

Before returning to Panaji, beach lovers might wish to take a detour west from Goa Velha. There is a dark sand beach shaded with palms at **Bambolim** where an up-market beach resort, the Cidade de Goa, has a pleasant terrace restaurant. Check out **Siridao Beach** if all you want is a stroll by the sea or to collect the pretty **shells** that often wash ashore here. (They are used to make traditional 'carepa' windows, still seen in old Goan houses.)

Chorao and Divar Islands

Between Panaji and Old Goa, there are views of the two islands in the Mandovi – Chorao and Divar. **Chorao** is approached by ferry (every 15 minutes, 6am–10pm) from **Ribander** (5km/3 miles east of Panaji). Before you leave, it is well worth checking out an upmarket boutique called

Camelot (9.30am–6.30 pm, closed Sunday). Fine cotton and linen furnishing fabrics, Indian designer fashions, furniture, lamps and decorative crafts are well displayed in the renovated salons of an old villa facing the waterfront (the shop entrance is along a narrow bend on the main road).

General store and local kids on Chorao

Once on Chorao the road leads north to the charming village of ★ **Chorao**, with a white church and some Portuguese-style villas. The northern part of the island is connected to Naroa *(see Route 6, page 49)* via a bridge and there is also a ferry crossing point here for Divar Island.

Just 2 sq km (1 sq mile) of Chorao's western flank is occupied by the ★ **Dr Salim Ali Bird Sanctuary** (9am–5pm; best in winter or early spring). The mangroves along the river are home to a large variety of waterfowl, including grey and purple herons, pintails, snipes and terns, madder ducks and blue-winged teals. The river teems with freshwater crabs and mud skippers – a variety of fish that are able to breathe through their mouths and look out for predators with their roving eyes. They move about in mud with a curious skip-jump action. The sanctuary has no roads and can be visited only by boat. Some official tours are bookable through travel agents, but there are plenty of private fishing boats that will take on passengers.

From Old Goa, a ferry boat (every 15 minutes, 6am–10pm) near the Viceregal Arch runs to the south of **Divar Island**. The only other approach to this island is from Naroa *(see above)*. The main village of ★ **Piedade** nestles at the foot of a hill in a green valley and is dominated by its 18th-century Church of Our Lady of Compassion. There are lovely old villas and mansions in the Portuguese-Goan style, complete with deep-covered balconies. Each January the menfolk – who often work abroad – return home and parade the flags of their adopted countries during the Bandeira festival, while prospective brides look them over.

Divar Island

Ponda paddy fields

Cinnamon

Route 3

Spices and temples

Panaji via Old Goa – Kundai (Sinai Kundaiker House – Priol (Manguesh Temple) – Mardol (Mahalsa Temple) – Velinga (Lakshmi Narcenha Temple) Farmaguddi – Ponda (Safa Masjid) – Shri Naguesh Temple –Mahalakshmi Temple – Shri Shantadurga Temple – Durbhat – Agapur (58 km/ 36 miles) *See map on pages 26–7*

This route crosses a charming rural landscape of lush paddy fields and palm trees to the predominantly Hindu district of Ponda. The scenic landscape of low hills and forested valleys crossed by rivers and streams is famed for spice plantations and Goan Hindu architecture. Seven temples lie within a 5-km (3-mile) radius of Ponda town.

Temple offerings at Priol

Located south of the Zuari River, this densely wooded inland region was not considered of much economic value by successions of rulers. Hindus brought their precious deities here with them and found clandestine sites to rebuild temples when the Inquisition of the 17th and 18th centuries outlawed their religion and destroyed the original shrines along the coastal belt. Unlike most other Hindu temples, the ones near Ponda are located in solitary spots close to a fresh-water source which supplies the temple tank.

Pilgrims from neighbouring states come here regularly as do the local Hindus, particularly during temple festivals when the deities are carried through the streets on special ceremonial chariots – called *rathas* – accompanied by devotees.

Commercial **spice plantations** that dot the area sometimes offer guided tours and, for a nominal fee, one can see how spices like cardamom, cinnamon and nutmeg are grown among tropical fruits ranging from pineapples, papayas, and bananas to jackfruit and mangoes. You can sample local food and drink made from the fresh fruit and spices. It makes a pleasant change from temple-touring. (For bookings, contact Tropical Spice Plantation Rohidas Satarkar, A-14 Arla Bazaar, Ponda, tel: 0832-234 0329; open daily 8am–6pm – *also see over page, and Route 4, page 36.*)

National Highway 4 from Panaji takes 28km (17 miles) to reach Ponda. First loop past Old Goa towards **Kundai** (3km/1¾ miles northwest of Mardol), where a quick stop can be made in the areca palm grove to see a 250-year-old Hindu mansion. Known as the ★ **Sinai-Kundaiker House**, the striking entrance is heavily fortified, and holes are drilled for rifle muzzles beside the metal doors at the end of a narrow hallway. The grand salon was redecorated around 1900 and features a high ceiling and walls painted with tropical landscapes and unusual allegorical murals. The ancestor who was knighted by the Portuguese has his portrait most prominently displayed.

Sinai-Kundaiker House

33

Stop next at **Priol**, 9km (5½ miles) north of Ponda, to visit the well-known **Manguesh Temple**, set amid lush forests below a steep hill. The original deity was brought here in the 16th century from Cortalim and the temple is a typical example of Goan architectural fusion. The large complex houses the usual pilgrims' quarters, administrative offices and ceremonial halls. There are a variety of smaller shrines besides the main sanctum and a rather murky water tank out in front. One can also glimpse the gaudy temple chariots used during the annual festival held in late January or early February.

Manguesh Temple

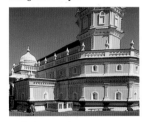

Another remarkable temple lies only 1km (½ mile) south at **Mardol**. Dedicated to an unusual incarnation of Vishnu, the ★ **Mahalsa Temple** has a particularly peaceful compound. Red-tiled roofs, beautiful carved wooden pillars and slatted windows set off a seven-storey lamp tower with a massive brass oil lamp . A winged garuda on a brass pillar mounted on the back of a turtle is awe-inspiring. There are also some brightly painted carvings of the 10 incarnations of Vishnu. Mahalsa, also known as Mohini, is considered a female form of Vishnu – and the most beautiful woman ever created. In order to distract his enemies, the deity would sometimes appear in her guise. The big annual festival is held in February, but two minor festivals are usually are held during August and September.

Mahalsa Temple

Just south of Mardol, turn right onto the side road leading uphill for 3km (2 miles) to the serene **Lakshmi**

Acrobatics at Savoi Verem

Narcenha Temple at **Velinga**. This place is dedicated to the fourth incarnation of Vishnu, in which he adopts the unusual form of a half-lion and half-man (Narasimha). Originally, the deity was housed in a temple in Salcete *taluka* which was destroyed in 1567 by a Portuguese commander of Rachol Fort who was notorious for obliterating more than 50 Hindu temples in Goa. The present temple was built in the 18th century in the Goan style, but has an unusual Islamic-style dome and tower.

Near the entrance is a palm-bordered water tank fed by springs. The tower rising behind it was once a musicians' gallery. Finely carved wooden pillars support the roof, and the principal shrine is hidden behind a silver screen.

Farmaguddi, 4km (2½ miles) north of Ponda, has a decent GTDC Tourist Resort with pleasant chalets situated on the slopes of a hill overlooking the highway. It also has a small terrace restaurant with distant views. This makes a good overnight base to explore the area. Visiting a **spice plantation** like the one at ★ **Savoi Verem**, 10km (6 miles) northeast of Ponda, makes for a pleasant and interesting afternoon diversion (tel: 0832-234 0272; www.savoi-plantation.com; open daily 7am–6pm; or Sahakari Spice Farm, 1km east of Ponda on National Highway 4A, tel: 0832-231 2394; open daily 8am–6pm; www.sahakari-farms.com; or Tropical Spice Plantation, *see page 33*).

Although **Ponda** was once heavily fortified and set up as the base for a rebellion by Adil Shah's brother, Abdullah, in 1555, the revolt never took place. All this area remained under Islamic control, and the town's famous old mosque, the Safa Masjid, was constructed at leisure. Eventually, the defiant Maratha leader, Shivaji, conquered this entire zone and it remained a Hindu district on the borders of the Portuguese colony, separated by the river which formed a natural border until 1791. The Hindu King of Sunda surrendered it to the Portuguese – together with Sanguem, Canacona and Quepem – and it became a part of their New Conquests.

Continue through **Ponda** town and drive 2km (1¼ miles) east in Shapur District to reach Goa's oldest mosque – the ★ **Safa Masjid**, built in 1560 by Adil Shah of Bijapur. The building has a simple exterior marked by Bijapuri-style arches and is often locked. An ancient laterite water tank in front is said to have underwater tunnels that connect it to a nearby reservoir. It was once surrounded by extensive gardens with ornate fountains, which were all destroyed by the marauding Marathas and Portuguese.

Next, follow the narrow back road from Farmaguddi intersection. It winds sharply down the slopes of valley rich with cashew trees and palm groves and leads to the **Shri Naguesh Temple** at **Bandora**, 4km (2½ miles) west

Safa Masjid

of Ponda. The temple is dedicated to an incarnation of Shiva. The main sanctum here houses the deity with Lakshmi Narayan on a lotus flower to his left and elephant-headed Ganesh to the right. Another shrine on the south side of the compound venerates a rare form of the god – Mukhalinga – a lingam carved with the face of Shiva. Colourful wooden carvings in the main hall depict scenes from the Sanskrit epics, *Ramayana* and *Mahabharata*, and show the the eight directional guardians of Hinduism, known collectively as the Ashtadikpalas. Indra, Agni, Yama, Nirriti, Varuna, Vayu, Kubera and Ishana are carefully incised. Outside, near a stand of palm trees, is a large temple tank, enclosed by laterite walls. Greenish water teems with fat carp that are fed by visiting pilgrims. An annual festival is celebrated in November during full moon.

Just to the south, situated in a lush valley, is the **Mahalakshmi Temple**. It is a centre of ancient female power, the principal Shakti cult at Bandora. The deity assumes her original form here – and although she wears a phallus-like lingam on her head, she is considered a peaceful form of the goddess. Also remarkable are the 22 wooden statues of Vishnu housed in the assembly hall.

Shri Shantadurga Temple

Drive 3km (2 miles) southwest of Ponda to reach Goa's largest and most renowned shrine – the ★★★ **Shri Shantadurga** (Goddess of Peace) Temple, built by the Marathas in the 1730s. It is set on the slopes of a hill surrounded by forests at **Quela**. Steep steps lead up to the main entrance, surrounded by newly built administrative buildings and pilgrim hostels. Expect crowds, since this is a popular destination for pilgrims. Marble interiors are lit up by lavish chandeliers and in the main sanctum, behind a silver screen, is Shiva's consort Parvati – flanked by Shiva and Vishnu. The temple is dedicated to the Peaceful Durga – a title the powerful tiger-riding goddess was given when she mediated in a quarrel between these two gods and pacified them. The idol of the goddess was brought here 200 years ago from Quelossim.

Each January, this temple is opened for one day to the lower castes (who are normally denied entry). It is then ceremonially purified next day. The annual festival is usually held around mid-February, depending on the moon.

If you have time, continue southwest following the river to **Durbhat**, which used to be a port before the Zuari silted up. Visit a trio of 11th-century shrines erected on a low hill at nearby **Agapur**. The blocks of laterite have been fitted together without mortar and date from the time when carpenters would work as stonemasons in Hindu temples. Impressive domes are well-preserved beneath a new tiled roof and are very similar to the North Indian style.

A family group

Head to head near Colem

Route 4

A tour on the wild side

Ponda – Khandepar (Buddhist Rock-cut Cave Temples) – Spice Plantation – Bondla Wildlife Sanctuary – Molem – Bhagwan Mahaveer Wildlife Sanctuary – Colem Railhead for Dudhsagar Falls – Tambdi Surla Temple (57 km/35 miles) *See map on pages 26–7*

This route goes deep inland through Ponda district via some ancient Buddhist ruins at Khandepar. After visiting a spice farm in the vicinity, stop at the tiny Bondla Sanctuary, then cross the border into Sanguem, to reach Bhagwan Mahaveer Sanctuary and a stunning waterfall.

Rock-cut temples at Khandepar

From Ponda, head 5km (3 miles) northeast on National Highway 4 to **Khandepar** village. Hidden amid a forest and near a tributary of the Mandovi River are Goa's oldest historical monuments dating back to to the first century. Four free-standing ★ **rock-cut cave temples** are believed to be Buddhist in origin. Their simple two cells are hewn out of laterite. Their more elaborate tiered roofs were added considerably later – around the 10th and 11th centuries – by the Hindu Kadambas. Inside, there are niches in the walls once used for oil lamps and assorted pegs for hanging clothes, probably used by resident Buddhist monks. The site is difficult to find without a local guide (ask at the crossroads).

Nearby are **Pascoal Farms**, 8km (5 miles) from Ponda, just off the main road. This riverside spice plantation is open to visitors (tel: 9422 055455; www.pascoalspice-village.com; daily 8.30am–5.30pm). Guided tours are as informative as they are fragrant. There is a pleasant bar and restaurant, and paddle-boats and fishing lines are for hire. Gift-packs of fresh spices can be bought here.

Continue east on National Highway 4 for 6km (4 miles) to the village of **Tisk**, which is the departure point for the Forest Department's special minibus service (Monday, Wednesday, Friday and Saturday: 11am and 7pm; Sunday: 10.30am and 7pm) to the ★★ **Bondla Wildlife Sanctuary** (mid-September to mid-June, 9am–5pm, closed Thursday). This game reserve offers 8 sq km (3 sq miles) of spectacular scenery, luxuriant forests and hills where Indian bison, monkeys, jackals, wild boar, deer, pythons and some elusive leopards make their home.

If you have your own transport, you may alternatively turn north before reaching Tisk, onto National Highway 4 towards Usgao village and enter by the western gate. Inside there is a café and car park. Information can be obtained at the small **Nature Interpretation Centre** (daily except Thursday 9.30am–1pm and 2pm–5.30pm). The Zoological and Botanical Gardens offer elephant rides and a chance to see caged jungle cats and other captive animals. The only accommodation here is in wooden tourist cottages, operated by the Forest Department, which have simple en-suite double rooms and dorm beds. Book in advance direct with the guest house (tel: 222 9701) or via the Forest Department office in Panaji (tel: 222 4747).

A scenic short-cut from here leads to the adjoining Bhagwan Mahaveer Sanctuary *(see below)* via a lane heading south from the car park – however, it involves fording several streams and is closed during the monsoon.

A rare gaur bison at Bondla Wildlife Sanctuary, and the Interpretation Centre (below)

The more usual route to this sanctuary follows National Highway 4 to **Molem**, where the Range Officer can be contacted at the Nature Interpretation Centre near the police checkpost for vehicle access keys for the main gate and for entry tickets. West of the park entrance is the GTDC Dudhsagar Resort (tel: 261 2238) with clean cottages, five-bedded dorms and a restaurant known more for its chilled beer than its food. From Colem Station, 5km (3 miles) to the south, jeeps depart for Dudhsagar Falls.

The ★★★ **Bhagwan Mahaveer Wildlife Sanctuary** (daily 9am–5pm) along the eastern border of Goa is the largest nature reserve in the state. It consists of 240 sq km (92 sq miles) of thick green forests and savannah grassland bounded by the foothills of the Western Ghats. All the way to the Karnataka border, thick evergreen and deciduous forests spread over low hills to the horizon. The area is home to the indigenous Dhangar tribe, who are permitted to forage and live off the land. Wild animals inhabiting the area include gaur bison, sambar deer, leopards, jungle cats, giant squirrels, pythons and cobras. The sanctuary is also

famous for the spectacular ★★ **Dudhsagar Falls** in its eastern corner, which can be approached only by private jeep, from **Colem**. The trip takes 30–40 minutes, following rough tracks, fording streams and winding up with a 15-minute hike up to the base of the splendid Falls.

There is the option of a short 10-km (6-mile) train journey to the Falls, which goes through stunning scenery – the line passes straight across the middle of the Falls – but services only run in one direction per day, making return trips impossible.

The name Dudhsagar in Konkani means 'Flow of Milk' and refers to the clouds of mist that form at the bottom after the monsoon. The headwaters of the Mandovi River churn through three streams that cascade 600m (1,900ft) down a steep cliff into a deep green pool at the base. The second highest falls in India, they are spanned by an old viaduct. To explore further, follow the tracks from the station platform, turn right after crossing a gap between two tunnels and negotiate a slippery path up to a shaded pool lined by large boulders.

Further downstream there are several secluded spots that are ideal for swimming or watching a variety of lovely butterflies and iridescent kingfishers. For superb views, hike up to the head of the Falls, a tough 90-minute climb which is worth the effort.

Organised trips to Dudhsagar, comprising transport to and from the falls, and meals, are run from most of Goa's main resorts. Look for ads on the roadsides and lanes leading to the beaches.

Tambdi Surla Temple

Twelve kilometres (7½ miles) north of Molem, after winding through sylvan stretches and a succession of villages, head for the atmospheric ★ **Tambdi Surla Temple**, the lone survivor of the Muslim and Portuguese campaign that defaced or destroyed all the other Hindu temples in Goa. This may have been because of its remote location amid thick jungles. To reach the temple, follow the north road towards Sancordem from the Molem crossroads, turning right towards Bolkonda after 3 km (1¾ miles). Continue for another 3km (1¾ miles) until the next fork, where a sign should point towards the car park for Tambdi Surla.

Dedicated to Shiva, the original shrine was built by the Kadambas around the 12th century from imported black basalt. This small temple has intricately carved bas-reliefs of the gods of the Hindu trinity – Shiva, Vishnu and Brahma – each with his respective consort. A delicate lotus motif decorates the ceiling of the main pillared porch and the stone screen which guards the shrine has four fine images of deities, including Ganesh, the elephant god of auspicious beginnings. Outside, old stone steps lead down towards the river to the east.

Route 5

Northern beaches and historic forts

Panaji – Betim – Reis Magos – Fort Aguada – Sinquerim – Candolim – Calangute – Baga – Arpora – Anjuna – Vagator – Chapora (35km/ 21 miles) *See map on page 40*

Singuerim Beach and children at Candolim

This route covers most of coastal North Goa within Bardez *taluka*. It goes past green rice paddies, coconut groves and fishing villages to stop at stalwart Portuguese forts and some of Goa's loveliest beaches.

Bardez forms part of Portugal's Old Conquests, first coming under colonial control in 1534. The name refers to the 12 Brahmin villages that once occupied this region and were linked to Govapuri. The Franciscan Order was permitted to base its operations in Bardez, and specialised in mass conversions. The latest wave of colonisation in the area has come from tourism. The fabulous coast – lined with golden beaches, sand dunes, and coconut groves between rocky headlands – is the one that first made Goa famous as a tourist destination. Until the 1970s, the beaches here were pristine and the sleepy villages had no tourist facilities – an untramelled haven for alternative travellers who preferred to come overland. But Goa's commercial potential was soon realised and with the first luxury resort near Fort Aguada, the tourist boom began to change the face of these modest villages.

Fresh construction is everywhere – particularly around Calangute. New resorts compete with hotels, restaurants, telephone booths, travel agencies, handicraft shops and vendors from different regions of India. The scramble for tourist rupees lasts roughly from November to February. The Anjuna flea market is held every Wednesday and the beaches are full of package tourists and revellers determined to party through the New Year. By mid-February, most of these tourists leave and the beaches become more peaceful.

One can walk almost continuously along the beaches from Aguada to Vagator, circling the headlands by little paths that pass many tiny bays formed by the rocks. There are ruined Portuguese forts at Reis Magos, Aguada and Chapora with their thick, wide stone walls, underground chambers and passages. There is no dearth of accommodation here and it makes a good base for visiting other sites and beaches in North Goa.

The tour starts at **Panaji** and goes across the Mandovi River Bridge, turning left onto a narrow coastal road to drive 1km (½ mile) towards **Betim** – a busy fishing village

Betim waterfront

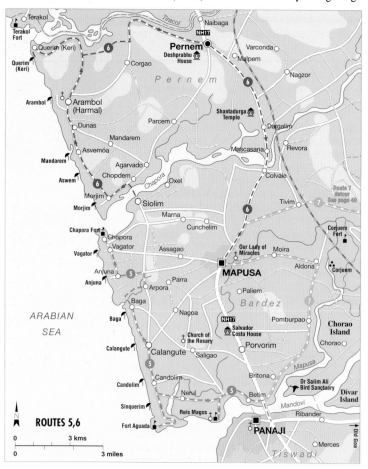

ROUTES 5,6

0   3 kms

0   3 miles

ARABIAN SEA

Map labels:
Terakol, Terakol Fort, Tiracol, Naibaga, Querim (Keri), Querim (Keri), Corgao, Pernem, Deshprabhu House, Varconda, Malpem, Nagzor, Arambol, Arambol (Harmal), Dunas, Parcem, Shantadurga Temple, Dargalim, Mandrem, Mandarem, Asvemóa, Mascasana, Revora, Aswem, Agarvado, Chopdem, Chapora, Oxel, Colvale, Morjim, Morjim, Siolim, Tivim, Marna, Cunchelim, Route 7 detour See page 49, Chapora Fort, Chapora, Vagator, Vagator, Assagao, Our Lady of Miracles, Moira, Corjuem Fort, Anjuna, Parra, MAPUSA, Aldona, Corjuem, Anjuna, Arpora, Baga, Nagoa, Paliem, Bardez, Baga, NH17, Salvador Costa House, Pomburpao, Chorao Island, Calangute, Calangute, Church of the Rosary, Saligao, Porvorim, Chorao, Candolim, Candolim, Britona, Dr Salim Ali Bird Sanctuary, Divar Island, Nerul, Mapusa, Sinquerim, Betim, Reis Magos, Mandovi, Ribander, Fort Aguada, PANAJI, Merces, Tiswadi, Old Goa

from where seafood is loaded into trucks and whisked off to cities inland.

Just west of the town bazaar, a road leads to the former village of Verem or **Reis Magos** and its fort, built in 1551 by the Portuguese to protect this narrowest part of the River Mandovi. Alfonso de Albuquerque had always recognised the strategic importance of this site, and though it fell into disuse after the construction of Fort Aguada, it was rebuilt later and used in the defence of Bardez against the Maratha attacks around 1738.

Just below the fort, one can see the white facade of the ★ **Reis Magos Church** which was built in 1555 on the site of an old Hindu temple. Franciscan friars opened a seminary here. The interior contains the tombs of three Portuguese viceroys. The magnificent carved and painted reredos behind the altar centre around a beautifully coloured depiction of the biblical **three wise men** (Magi) visiting the infant Jesus and bearing gifts of frankincense, myrrh and gold. During Epiphany in the first week of January, the scene is reenacted by three local boys during the Festa de Reis Magos. The church can be approached via steep laterite steps off the road. On the short scenic drive heading to the end of the peninsula, make sure you turn back before it gets too narrow.

Reis Magos Church

Once past the village of Nerul, turn left at the end of the road towards ★★ **Fort Aguada**, situated at the summit of a rocky headland overlooking the mouth of the River Mandovi, at **Sinquerim**. The fort is the largest and best preserved of the Portuguese forts still standing in Goa. At present, part of the fortress is used as a state prison, but there are plans afoot to convert it into a luxury resort. To reach it, follow the road uphill from the turning just east of the Aguada Hermitage Hotel which passes the small Church of St Lawrence. Built by the Portuguese early in the 17th century, the fort, with its thick laterite walls and defence of 200 guns and two magazines, came to be considered their strongest bastion, with the distinction of never having been conquered by invaders. It was named Aguada after the natural springs in the hillside which were an important watering point for Portuguese ships (as evidenced by the enormous size of the storage tanks beneath the main courtyard of the fort). A customised channel and disembarking platform were set up for the great frigates and galleons which would regularly dock here. The complex had four barracks and two prisons alongside residences for the officers.

Fort Aguada

There is an **old lighthouse** built in 1864 and it is well worth a visit for the panoramic **views** of the northern coast up to Vagator and of the Cabo Raj Nivas and Mormugao Harbour to the south. The **new lighthouse** nearby is Asia's biggest and can also be visited (daily 4–5.30pm). Another spot for good views is from the terrace outside the **Church of St Lawrence**, built in 1643. It is dedicated to this patron saint of sailors whose statue – holding a model ship – can be seen inside above the reredos behind the altar. It also has some unusual balustrades on the towers.

The coastal road continues past the lovely ★★ **Sinquerim Beach**, 13km (8 miles) from Panaji, with its luxury resorts – notably the Taj Hermitage (which adjoins the Fort). It has a modern sports complex (open to non-residents) and upmarket restaurants. The Banyan Tree Restaurant within the Taj Holiday Village Complex offers sumptuous Thai food in an exotic garden beside an ancient Banyan tree.

Café at Candolim

The next beach at **Candolim** has more accommodation and watersports facilities on a long shore lined with shacks that offer sun umbrellas and sun beds for hire. Diners linger over fresh fruit juices, fried snacks and sea-food.

Calangute

The lively tourist centre of **Calangute** is next on the route, with banks, a post office, a petrol pump, shops, travel agencies and roadside vendors hawking everything a tourist may need: all kinds of souvenirs, handicrafts, clothing, sandals, and earrings. There is even a little local fruit and vegetable market where the fisherwomen bring in the catch early in the morning.

The road to the next beach at **Baga**, 3km (2 miles) along, is lined with places to stay, restaurants, car and motorcycle rentals, plus telephone booths with internet facilities. The beachfront is crammed with restaurant shacks that whip up a milkshake or a fresh fruit juice and display the day's specials on a blackboard. Deckchairs and sun umbrellas can be rented and massages are popular.

Boats at Baga Beach

At Baga, **Tito's Restaurant & Bar** is a lively evening spot, or head for the well-established **St Anthony's** for sundowners. A small river separates the north end of the beach from the low hill beyond which lies Anjuna Beach. Tourist buses arrive at a square here at lunchtime or on Sundays bringing families and school groups for a stroll on the beach or a picnic lunch. At **Valerio's Restaurant** opposite the square, there is a pleasant terrace with sea views. Live music can be heard on Wednesday evenings.

An unpaved road crosses the river via an ugly concrete bridge (which can be difficult to negotiate on a motorbike). To the left the road dwindles to a track which leads past Sunset Bar and around the hill to Anjuna (45 minutes approximately). This makes for a very scenic walk past a couple of tiny, secluded bays, but is best attempted well before sunset. Watch out for snakes. Turning right off the bridge, the road leads to **Arpora** and joins the main road to Anjuna or Mapusa. A number of up-market, modern flats and resorts have sprung up here in recent years. This has also become the venue of a market held each Saturday evening during the season. But there's a second, and much superior, **night market** held another 3km (2 miles) along the main road. Named after its German organiser, Ingo's Bazaar is where most of the resident expats sell their designer beach wear and jewellery, alongside the usual gamut of Indian handicrafts. Arrive by 8pm when the live music starts up and musicians from different countries jam together.

Anjuna village comes next. The name seems to have been Muslim in origin – most likely 'Hanjuman', a wealthy Arab trading town. However, the place also had a Hindu population with their own Bhumika Devi Temple. It was obliterated by the Portuguese and replaced with the Church of St Michael. In 1628, there was a minor rebellion when the local villagers protested at the forced conversion by the parish priest of the child of a Hindu woman. She had escaped to the interior and returned with her newly born infant. The priest was injured in the fracas and the Portuguese retaliated harshly – executing those found guilty and confiscating their lands. A warning was inscribed onto a **rock pillar** which now lies broken in half in the vicinity of the Vagator petrol pump. This pillar is known as the **Morkachi Fator** (literally, 'accursed stone' in Konkani) and is considered a memorial to those who have the courage to stand up for their rights.

Anjuna flea market

Anjuna is now famous for its ★★ **flea market** held on Wednesdays near the southern end of the village, when this otherwise quiet area gets flooded with tourists from the rest of Goa (see Shopping, *page 78*). En route to the flea market stop at the big church square and check out the shops. Oxford and Orchard sells gourmet goods: cheeses, avocados, salad ingredients, fruit, groceries and a wide range of toiletries. Upstairs, browse at Walkabout bookshop, or try the boutique next door for some beachwear from Bali.

The nightspot for raves and trance is **Café de Paradiso** at the north end of the main beach. The only place said to have an official permit to play loud music, it is a concrete pavilion with steps down to a bay via a couple of terraces. There can be quite a scene here with *chai* sellers setting up rush mats for customers on the beachfront and slopes leading to it. Huge speakers pump out the Goa Trance music that originated here, as well as a range of techno and psychedelic dance played by popular DJs who have their own cult following. Black lights are obligatory.

Parties tend to go on until sunrise at least, sometimes continuing over a couple of days. If there is a party on elsewhere then this café may be the place to get directions. (Warning: drug laws have recently been relaxed in Goa, but possession of more than a gram of cannabis or an

ecstasy tablet is still a serious offence carrying a prison sentence.) Efforts have been made to keep the beachfront clean by providing rubbish bins marked for recycling.

On the road from Anjuna to Vagator, a scale model of Zanzibar palace was built at the turn of the century by a local doctor who for years served the Sultan of Zanzibar. After retirement, Dr Manuel Albuquerque was permitted to build a personal copy of the sultan's flamboyant residence in his own village. African materials and the services of craftsmen were donated and the whitewashed Moorish **Albuquerque House** can still be seen from the outside, although it is now a drug rehabilitation centre.

The next village north is **Vagator** with peaceful shaded lanes and some old Portuguese villas. There are plenty of places to stay, tucked away in the leafy lanes below Chapora Fort and behind Vagator's main beach, Big Vagator. Two other lovely coves lie to the south, **Ozran** and **Little Vagator**. These can be approached by a steep path down from the lane near the Alcove Restaurant. There is a sculpted Shiva here carved in the natural rock and a freshwater spring trickles into a shaded pool.

Chapora is a bustling fishing and boat-building village with its own jetty. The village houses are half-hidden among trees south of a beautiful river estuary. There is no beach here, but the area is ideal for walking or cycling. Stunning views along the estuary attract couples at sunset. There are several popular juice bars and cafés in the village, which is dominated by a fortress more easily reached from the Vagator side of the hill. This red laterite fortress was built in 1617 on the site of an earlier Muslim structure and was abandoned by the Portuguese in 1892. Although in ruins, it is still worth a visit for the superb **views** north to Morjim and Mandarem and south to Anjuna.

Chapora

Big Vagator Beach

Route 6

Goa's northernmost beaches

Siolim – Morjim – Mandarem – Arambol/Harmal – Querim/Keri Beach – Terekhol Fort – Pernem (Deshprabhu House) – Shantadurga Temple near Dargalim/Dhargal – Colvale – Mapusa – Guerim (55 km/34 miles) *See map on page 40*

This route covers most of Pernem *taluka* – the district that lies furthest north in Goa and shares the border with the neighbouring state of Maharashtra. It was a part of the New Conquests: lush forests and paddy fields watered by the Tiracol River. Exquisite beaches fringed with palms skirt sleepy villages at Morjim, Mandarem and Arambol. Mangroves tangle beneath Keri and Terekhol Fort.

At Pernem, the district headquarters, one can visit Goa's grandest Hindu family mansion: the Deshprabhu House. Return through Mapusa, capital of Bardez *taluka* and a busy town famous for its Friday market where hawkers sell everything, including fresh farm products, vegetables and fruit and jewellery. A detour to Guerim to visit a stately ancestral home is possible before returning to a beach resort or Panaji.

This route starts at **Siolim**, where the attractive local Church of St Anthony (1606) stands at the main square. Just 1km (½ mile) north is the new road bridge, from where a left turn leads to peaceful **Morjim** village at the mouth of the Chapora River estuary. The Shri Morja Devi Temple here is notable for a shrine dedicated to a Jain teacher, which suggests an ancient origin (perhaps as early as the 6th century). Take the narrow road which skirts the estuary, with fine views of Chapora Fort, to where the river joins the sea. Morjim has a beautiful, long white ★ **beach** which stretches nearly 3km (2 miles) north to Asvem.

Siolim ferry
Rural help at Morjim

The road to the village turns sharply inland and goes up through some low hills. A turn-off before the village leads to **Asvem**, which has a serene shorefront with palm trees, food shacks and some beach huts to let.

At **Mandarem**, hidden amid palms beyond sand dunes, there are a few houses with rooms to let near a quiet beach. Mandarem has an unusual medieval statue of Garuda (the vehicle of Vishnu) where the winged half-man/half-eagle *vahana* is shown suited in a soldier's uniform, ready for battle. The road to **Arambol/Harmal** crosses the plateau, through cashew groves, past the village crossroads and 500m (¼ mile) further to the beachfront. This was once a

Look out for the Arambol mud

Querim Beach

quiet fishing village with two very attractive beaches – one with a natural freshwater pool backing the bay. Fed by hot sulphur springs, the pool has a yellow mud which is said to make an extremely healthy body-pack. Frequently, mustardy muck plasters the swimmers lounging around the pool.

With the tourist boom at Calangute, this area became a refuge for the Goa 'old-timers' and backpackers in search of peace. However, the boom is already reaching here with plans for resort development and every year the number of day-trippers visiting from other beaches increases. There are plenty of beach shack cafés and places to eat besides accommodation for long-stay visitors. From the main beach, a track circles the headland, past several small bays to the smaller beach which offers paragliding facilities beside the freshwater lake and sulphur springs.

To reach **Querim/Keri Beach** on the south bank of the Terekhol River, either walk to the north of the second beach and follow a path over the headland or take the scenic drive along the Arondem River. Next to the ferry crossing to Terekhol Fort (ferry service every half hour, 6am–9.30pm, 15-minute trip) there is a deserted beach backed by fir trees which is good for sunbathing or a swim (warning: there are dangerous currents near the mouth of the estuary, so keep to the southern end of the beach for safe swimming).

Across the river, the tiny ★★ **Terekhol Fort** and **Portuguese chapel** make a stunning tableau. The complex has been converted to a smart hotel, the Fort Tiracol (tel: 226 8258), which enjoys splendid views down the coast. Its owners have tried to preserve the period feel of the place with traditional Portuguese colour schemes and antique furniture. The fort occupies the northernmost tip of Goa

Terekhol view

and was built by the Marathas in the 17th century. Captured by the Portuguese in 1746, it was re-named Holy Trinity following the viceroy's decision to erect the Chapel of St Anthony. There was a disturbing mass murder here in 1835 when, during a military revolt, the entire garrison were beheaded by a ruthless rebel commander alongside hapless civilians who were sheltering here. Some locals swear it's haunted.

In later years, the fort's distance from the capital made it a popular spot for Goan freedom fighters. They managed to enter the premises and raised the Indian flag on 15 August (the anniversary of Indian Independence) in 1954. Inside the chapel is a tiny gallery for the choir and two remarkable confessional chairs with small wooden extensions that provided a temporary screen between the priest and the sinner. The reredos above the altar feature St Anthony. There are some excellent panoramic views from the battlements and turrets and the terrace on the southern side of the fort.

Return to Querim and head east to the outskirts of **Pernem** town where one can visit the grand Hindu mansion – ★ **Deshprabhu House**. It was built by wealthy landowners who were allowed to keep their property after independence because they had helped India against Portugal, and is open to visitors. To avoid disappointment, it's best to make an appointment through a GTDC office or hotel. Within its numerous wings and 16 courtyards is a temple for the family deity and a small portrait gallery-cum-museum with some family heirlooms.

Pernem local and Deshprabhu House

North of town the road rejoins National Highway 17 and the route continues south past the **Shantadurga Temple** near Dargalim/Dhargal,14km (8 miles) north of Mapusa. To visit the shrine, turn off through a large gate onto a side road that leads to the main entrance (500m/¼ mile).

The fishing village of **Colvale**, 2km (1¼ miles) south, shows traces of early Buddhist influences, since one of its oldest deities is named Gautama and an ancient statue of Buddha (2nd century) was found nearby. The local Church of St Francis of Assisi has an attractive facade with a fine statue of the saint.

Cross the bridge here over the Chapora River and continue south. **Mapusa** is the headquarters and transport hub of Bardez *taluka*. It is located in a fertile valley that was formerly swampland (*Maha apsa* or great swamps), and is a good place to spend some time. There is a wide range of accommodation at the North Goa beach resorts (a 20-minute drive).

The local church, ★ **Our Lady of Miracles** (1594), is said to be dedicated to a Hindu woman who converted to Christianity. This small building with an interesting

Mapusa: the Friday Market

facade and wooden ceiling inside was rebuilt after a fire in 1839 and is on the site of the Hindu Shanteri Temple, making it a pilgrimage spot for both communities. The annual *festa* is held on the Monday of the third week after Easter and is celebrated by a large gathering of Christian and Hindu pilgrims.

Friday Market

The other attraction here is the ★★ **Friday Market**, where a wide range of fresh fruits, vegetables and other products, including specialities like home-made Goan *chourico* (spicy sausages) and bottles of *feni* (a local brew made of coconut or cashew juice) are brought into town by vendors. Many are local housewives and fisherwomen from neighbouring towns and villages who set up stalls around the Municipal Market (8am–6pm, closed Sunday) which is almost as colourful. A good spot for book lovers is the Other India Bookstore (above Mapusa Clinic) which has a wide range of books on Goa and India plus sundry other Asian, African and Latin American publications.

A recommended café-restaurant is FR Xavier's in the main market area, where you can eat delicious beef or vegetable 'patties' – a favourite Goan snack – washed down with chilled Kingfisher lager.

About 4km (2½ miles) south of Mapusa on the main road Porvorim is **Guerim**, where the ★ **Salvador Costa House** is well worth a visit. The whitewashed 18th-century mansion was built by a Portuguese civil servant. A chapel on the ground floor has a remarkable Gothic-style altar and in the entrance hall has an unusual stairway hewn out of a solid granite block. It opens onto a grand salon with painted ceilings and elegant antique furniture made of carved teak. The original kitchens, although hardly in use, still have some copper cauldrons and other utensils.

Extended family

Route 7

Into the interior

Sirigao – Sri Saptakoteshwar Temple – Mayem Lake – Sanquelim (Vitthala and Dattar Mandir Temples) – Arvalem –Valpoi – Carambolin (Brahma Temple) – detour to Moira – Aldona – Corjuem Fort – Britona (121 km/ 75 miles) *See map below and on page 40*

Recreation on Mayem Lake

This route goes through the interior districts of Bicholim and Satari *talukas*. Part of the New Conquests, the forested hills between the Mandovi and Mapusa Rivers provided shelter to Hindus who fled with their sacred idols to hide from the Inquisition. Centuries before the Portuguese, this sacred region was inhabited by Buddhists and Jains.

The route takes an entire day to complete, despite the short distances. It goes deep into the Satari district up to Carambolim and turns back to Mapusa from where a scenic detour along the river goes through Bardez district up to the Mandovi Bridge near Porvorim.

First head towards Sirigao/Shirgaum, about 5km (3 miles) northwest of Bicholim, to visit the ★ **Lairaya Temple** which is famous for ritual **fire-walking** during the festivities that begin on the first day of the Hindu New Year. The procession culminates with devotees walking over red hot coals from a specially constructed pyre of firewood.

Across the river from Divar Island at **Naroa** is one of the principal sights of Bicholim *taluka* – the tiny ★★ **Shri Saptakoteshwar Temple**. Well hidden amid trees, it was built in 1668 under the orders of the great Maratha leader Shivaji, when the deity was brought here from its original temple in Divar, which had been destroyed by the Portuguese. The temple has a simple exterior with a red-tiled roof, painted exterior walls and a Nandi bull facing the shrine that houses the sacred deity – a faceted Dharalinga.

Shri Saptakoteshwar Temple in Naroa

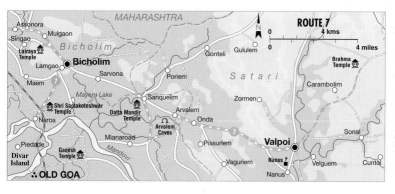

Mayem Lake
Vitthala Temple at Sanquelim

An elaborate Mahashivratri festival is celebrated here each year by pilgrims who arrive from distant villages for night-long festivities and prayer.

Stick to the country roads to bypass the district capital at Bicholim. It may be worth your while stopping at **Mayem Lake**, whose tourist complex includes a restaurant, bar, cottages and boating facilities, particularly since there are not many other such options available in the interior villages and towns further east.

The next sizeable town after Bicholim is **Sanquelim**, home to the migrant Rajasthani Rane tribe – former mercenary warriors who settled here in the late 18th century. Their north-Indian style ★ **Vitthala Temple** was built in the 14th century and is dedicated to their ancestral deity. Rane clan descendants still reside in their family home next to the temple. The **Datta Mandir**, built in 1882, draws supplicants who come from great distances to worship. Inside its white marble interior is a three-faced image of a deity, Dattarata, believed to cure insanity and multiple personality disorders. The atmosphere inside can seem highly charged or serene.

About 2km (1¼ miles) east of this temple, a turn to the south leads towards the small hamlet of **Arvalem** where there are some ★ **cave temples** from the 3rd century (see Architecture, *page 69*). These cells, with distinctive pillared porches, were hewn from solid laterite using very basic tools. Buddhist relics are conspicuous by their absence, and the caves now house shiva lingams instead.

Nearby, **waterfalls** cascade down to the base of a Shiva temple, where the Mahashivratri festival is celebrated with songs, processions and dramas, usually in late February. Steps from the parking area go down to the falls and a path continues along the river and across a footbridge to a **mine** about 1km (½ mile) away.

Mahashivratri festival, Arvalem

Valpoi is the district headquarters of Satari *taluka*, but the only accommodation available to tourists is a simple Forest Rest House that can be booked in advance from the Wildlife Office at Panaji (tel: 0832-224747/225926).

At **Carambolim**, 9km (5½ miles) northeast of Valpoi, a ★ **Brahma Temple** houses a unique and extremely finely wrought image of this powerful creator deity, who is rarely depicted. It dates back to the 5th century and is well worth a visit by connoisseurs of sacred imagery or fine art.

From Valpoi, the route turns back on the road to Bicholim and Mapusa *(see Route 6, page 47)*, where one can stay overnight.

Detour to the Mandovi Bridge *See map on page 40*

From Mapusa it is possible to take a short detour through some interesting places in interior parts of Bardez *taluka* towards the Mandovi Bridge across from Panaji, at which point one has a choice of returning to Mapusa or the northern beaches, or crossing the bridge and entering Panaji.

Moira church

51

Leaving Mapusa, travel along the Mapusa River past **Moira**, 5km (3 miles) to the east. The town dates from the 6th century when it was occupied by high-caste Brahmins who erected several important temples here. The Portuguese conducted a series of mass baptisms and, while some Hindus fled with their deities to Bicholim, others stayed in place and were converted. The impressive local ★ **Church of Our Lady Of the Immaculate Conception** was built in 1636. Despite modern renovations, it's worth stopping to view the unusual facade with square towers and a false dome, long balustrades and a bell transported from an abandoned church in Old Goa.

Further east, **Aldona** village is the ferry point for a visit to **Corjuem Fort** on the far side of Corjuem Island. This ruined military fortress with thick walls on a strategic hillock was built around 1705 and later abandoned by the Portuguese. One of the occupants of this remote outpost was an adventurous Portuguese woman, Ursula e Lancastre, who disguised herself as a man, travelled the world and ended up becoming a soldier posted here. Discovered when she was captured in an attack on the fort, she is said to have married a navy captain and resumed living as a woman again.

Corjuem Fort

To the south is **Pomburpao** village where the **Church of Nossa Senora Mae Deus** has an exceptional interior with rich reredos. Further along, at **Britona** village, is a church with an unusually high vaulted ceiling – **Our Lady of the Rock of France**.

At the junction of the Mandovi and Mapusa rivers across from Chorao Island, rejoin National Highway 17 and either cross the Mandovi Bridge back to Panaji or turn right towards Mapusa and the north coast.

Britona church

Bogmalo Beach Resort

Route 8

Time out for good manors

Dabolim – Bogmalo – Mormugao – Dona Paula – Sao Jacinto Island – Lutolim – Ancestral Goa – Rachol Fort and Seminary – Margao – Chandor – Zambaulim – Rivona – Pandava Caves – Parvath Temple – Shri Chandreshwar Temple (56km/35 miles) *See map opposite*

Interesting in itself, this tour is also designed for the convenience of travellers who find themselves stuck at the airport because of delays or who arrive too late to head out very far. Spend a few hours or even days exploring the harbour, taking a ferry trip or checking out the beaches. Wander inland, away from the crowds, to visit some of Goa's traditional family manors, a seminary and hill temples.

Head for the nearest café

Originally built by the navy, **Dabolim airport** has become an international airport with a dozen weekly charter flights from Europe supplementing regular domestic services and links to the Gulf. It is located a mere 4km (2½ miles) from the nearest beach at **Bogmalo** in the southeast – a 10-minute trip will bring you to this pleasant, palm-fringed cove. As well as plenty of shack restaurants and cafés, Bogmalo has a number of places to stay and it makes a good base. Boat trips to the small islands can be arranged with local fishermen from the southern end of the beach.

Three kilometres (1¾ miles) to the west of the airport is the harbour at **Mormugao**. Just before this large commercial port, one can stop at Pilot Point and climb up to the ruins of **Mormugao Fort** for extensive views of the coast. The fort was built by the Portuguese around 1585 on a high bluff projecting into the sea. This was to be the site of their new capital, since the one at Old Goa was proving increasingly unsuitable. But, although the viceroy took up residence here for a few months, the new site was formally abandoned after a few years. Mormugao is now a major Indian port and there is a steady trade in iron ore.

From here one can take a pleasant ferry trip (45 minutes one way, departs five times a day, last departure at 5.15pm) to **Dona Paula** *(see Route 1, page 23)*. En route there are views of **Sao Jacinto Island** – a harbour landmark with an old Portuguese lighthouse. The island is also connected to the mainland by a narrow causeway and approachable by road from the town of **Vasco da Gama**, adjacent to Mormugao port. On the southern banks of the Zuari River, the island village has old colonial houses, a whitewashed chapel, a ruined lighthouse and a small church.

Sao Jacinto Island

For a change of pace, go sightseeing via Curtolim to **Lutolim** village, 10km (6 miles) northeast of Margao, where grand mansions built in the 18th century by wealthy Goan landowners take pride of place. Many of these homes were retained after independence and are graciously

53

Getting around Lutolim

Ancestral Goa exhibits

opened up for visitors with prior appointments. You can book through GTDC offices or local hotels –the quirky furnishings inside more than compensate the effort.

Beginning at the main square in front of the quaint local church one can stroll through this pleasant neighbourhood and see typical examples of Goan architecture – pillared porches with stone benches, pyramidical tiled roofs and details like the window panes made of the inner, opaque layer of carepa shells. The nearest and the most splendid example is the ★ **Miranda House** to the west of the square. This is the family seat of Goa's famous cartoonist, Mario Miranda. Built in the early 18th century, half-hidden by high walls and shrubbery now, this double-storeyed house with deep verandahs contains several apartments, a ground floor chapel, and a staircase that leads up to the banquet hall on the first floor which further opens into a library.

A little further on, the elegant **Salvador Costa House** epitomises colonial taste, with lovely stained-glass windows, a chapel with gilded walls and ivory statues (open for prayers at noon each day), mosaic floors, rosewood furniture including a carved four-poster bed, Cantonese porcelain and Bohemian glass chandeliers.

Another fine house is located south of the main square. The **Roque Caetan Miranda House** was built around 1815 and features a splendid salon on the first floor with antique furniture, chandeliers, polished wooden floors and fretted French windows that open onto a series of balconies with decorative wrought-iron balustrades.

Just outside Lutolim, heading east towards Ponda, the route passes a kitschy outdoor exhibition, ★ **Ancestral Goa** (daily 9am–6pm). This is a time-warped diorama built by a local sculptor, Maendra Alvares, who lives alongside his creation. His model village features miniature versions of local houses and people at work in a way that reflects Goan lifestyles during the 19th century. Set amid spice and fruit gardens and a teak plantation, the conducted tour is a pleasant and informative experience. There are models of fishermen's bamboo and palm huts, a Portuguese taverna and even a scale model of an Iberian-style mansion. Every effort has been made to remain authentic in every detail. The other highlight of the exhibition is an enormous laterite sculpture by Alvares, depicting the legendary devotee of Krishna, Sant Mirabai, with her *ektara* – a one-stringed Indian musical instrument. Beyond this is a dance floor in the form of a Big Foot. This can be hired for private parties. There is also a shop with local handicrafts and pottery.

Opposite the main entrance, the site's owners have opened their ancestral family home to the public. **Casa Aranjo Alvares** has largely been stripped of its original furniture, but the guided tour is lovely.

Next on the route is **Rachol Fort and Seminary** – a gateway and ruined walls are all that remain of this former fort. However, the seminary established in 1580 is well maintained and still houses a college for priests, a hospital, a primary school, a library of rare books and large galleries. The **church** (open for daily services at 7am and 9am–1pm, 2.30pm–5pm) dates back to 1609 and has an impressive interior with nine altars, one of which has the statue of Menino Jesus, originally from Colva.

Rachol church: interior

Rachol Seminary

At this point, one can go directly to Margao and stay the night in order to explore further inland the next day, or head for Chandor and Paroda before returning.

Margao, the capital of Salcete *taluka* and the second largest city after Panaji, is a major transport hub. The station for the new broad-gauge and Konkan Railway that connects the state to the rest of the country is to the south. The Old Market Square or **Largo de Igreja** is notable for the baroque Church of the Holy Spirit and some fine 18th-century houses, notably the ★ **House of Seven Gables** owned by the da Silva family since 1790. Only five of the original seven towers which gave the house its name still stand. Inside, there is a wealth of carved rosewood furniture, chandeliers, gilded mirrors and oyster-shell window panes and outside is a pretty garden courtyard.

Officialdom in Margao

Walk (approx. 15 minutes) or drive up to Monte Hill, east of the square, for pleasant views over the town and coastal belt with its canopy of palms and green rice fields. The more energetic can visit the colourful municipal market (8am–1pm, 4–8pm, except Sunday), selling spices, grains, fruits, vegetables and all kinds of household gadgets.

Chandor lies 13km (8 miles) east of Margao in Salcete district and was the former capital of the Hindu Kadambas, ancient Chandrapura, said to date back to the 6th or 7th century. There is an impressive old manor opposite the

Menezes-Braganza House: chandeliers

church square. Known as the ★★**Menezes-Braganza House**, it belonged to a former freedom fighter who became a well-known journalist and politician, Luis de Menezes-Braganza (1878–1938). The best feature of this grand mansion (9am–6pm, tel: 278 4227) is a magnificent ballroom with Belgian chandeliers and mirrors, Italian marble floors and walls. Further highlights include an exquisite Chinese porcelain collection in the dining room and a chapel with a number of sacred relics such as a jewelled fingernail of St Francis Xavier on the main altar.

A detour from here goes south into Sanguem *taluka* towards the foothills of the Western Ghats and a further 7km (4 miles) to **Zambaulim**. Non-Hindus are welcome to visit **Shri Damodar Temple**, dedicated to Shiva, an important pilgrim centre. The temple looks modern because of extensive renovation, but the location is awe-inspiring. Saffron-clad sadhus, the wandering ascetics who renounce material life, frequently meditate here in the lotus position.

At **Rivona**, just 2km (1¼ miles) southeast, go past the tiny, isolated hamlet in the midst of forested hills. In the woods are two ancient rock-cut caves believed to have been made by Buddhist monks. Possibly dating from the 7th century, these are known as the ★**Pandava Caves** and show some later Hindu influence with carvings of Hanuman, the monkey deity, from the 16th century. Take a local guide and a torch if you plan to explore.

Continue 16km (10 miles) south from Rivana through the hamlet of Colomba and you'll arrive at a circular red, white and green sign pointing right. This indicates the way, down a rough dirt track, to the extraordinary **Usgalimal rock carvings**. Archaeologists only recently discovered the prehistoric site, which comprises around a dozen or more geometric shapes and distinct animal and human forms etched out of a laterite shelf beside a stream. The rock art is believed to date from the Upper Paleolithic or Mesolithic ages, 20,000 to 30,000 years ago, making this one of southern India's most significant archaeological sites.

Pandava Caves at Rivona

Chandreshwar Temple

The ★★**Shri Chandreshwar Temple** on **Chandranth Hill** at **Pardol/Paroda** is worth visiting just for the panoramic views, especially at sunset or during a full moon. Unlike many old Goan temple sites, tucked away for clandestine worship during the Inquisition, this one is situated atop a high peak, at an elevation of 370m (1,100ft). The hilly range rises abruptly off the coastal plains of Salcete *taluka*, and the Arabian Sea sparkles in the distance. This temple, dedicated to Shiva in his form of Chandreshwar (Lord of the Moon), is said to have existed here for 2,500 years. The present building dates back only as far as the 17th century, but the huge inner sanctum is believed to be part of the ancient original.

Route 9

Southern beaches and bays

Colva – Benaulim – Varca – Fatrade Beach – Cavelos-sim – Betul – Assolna – Cabo de Rama – Agonda – Palolem Bay – Colomb – Patnem – Rajbagh – Talpona – Galjibag – Mallikarjun Temple – Cotigao Wildlife Sanctuary – Partagali – Polem – detour to northern Karnataka (90km/54 miles) *See map on page 58*

This route follows the coastline of Salcete *taluka* to its southernmost point at Mobor and then moves into Canacona *taluka*, the last of Goa's New Conquests. The territory still retains its Hindu flavour. The coastal road from Colva passes a string of luxury hotels that dot Goa's exquisite southern beaches. Cross the Sal River at Cavelossim, and climb up the laterite headland to the ruined Portuguese fort at Cabo de Rama. The next district, Canacona, is set against spectacular rocky cliffs. Superb bays and beaches are backed by the wooded Sahyadri Hills. Or head inland towards the small Cotigao sanctuary for a day trip away from the coast.

Colva was one of the earliest seaside resorts in south Goa, popular with wealthy landowning families from Margao even during the Portuguese rule. There are several colonial-era villas scattered inland. The local **Church of Our Lady of Mercy** is famous for its miraculous Menino Jesus statue, which was found by a Jesuit priest in Mozambique during his journey to Goa where he arrived in 1648, setting up his rectory in Colva. The statue, supposedly endowed with miraculous healing power, drew many visitors until it was taken to Rachol Seminary in 1834 after a ban on

Aspects of Colva Beach

Family business

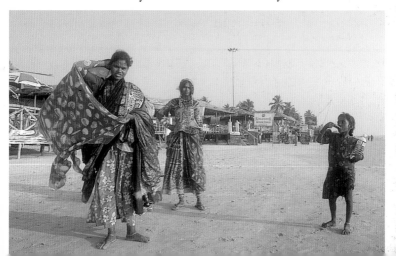

Shopping in Colva

religious orders. Thereafter, despite several requests, it was never returned and the present statue is only a replica. However, it wears a diamond and gold ring that dropped off the original and is said to have inherited all its miraculous powers. Meanwhile, the original statue is still at Rachol and seems to have lost its divine healing ability. Each year, on the second Monday in October, the statue is brought out of the vaults and displayed on a special altar after being taken for a ceremonial dip in the river. During **Menino Jesus Fama** thousands of pilgrims file past the statue, leaving curious petitions at the altar in the form of wax replicas of body parts that need healing.

Colva village is a convenient base for all Goa's southern beaches. It has travel agents, 24-hour ISD booths with fax, transport rental, shops and a wide range of accommodation. Numerous restaurants and bars provide some

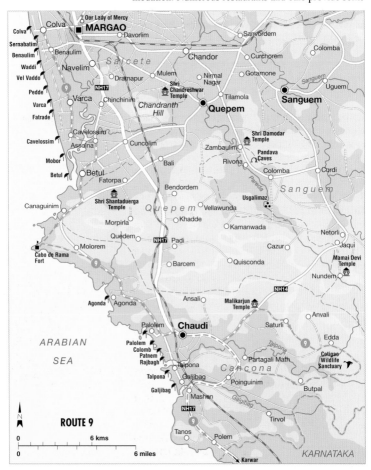

ROUTE 9

ARABIAN SEA

KARNATAKA

nightlife. The main beachfront is used as a tourist bus stop and the beach here is often dirty and crowded. Yet a short walk in either direction will get you to quiet, secluded spots for swimming and sunbathing. This splendid long beach is strewn with beautiful shells and shaded by coconut trees. **Dolphin spotting** day-trips by boat are on offer here and some stop at an island.

Beached at Varca

A pleasant way to get to ★ **Benaulim**, the next village south, is to walk or cycle the 4km (2½ miles) to this fishing centre. The village is an important site in Hindu mythology, being the epicentre of the creation myth of Goa when Lord Vishnu shot an arrow from the Western Ghats into the sea, and ordered the waters to recede. Benaulim in Sanskrit means *Banaliólit*, 'the place where the arrow fell'. Some new hotels have sprung up here recently as the village gears up for tourism, but it has a charming little church dedicated to **St John the Baptist**, built in 1596. The local *festa* is held on 24 June and is a thanksgiving for the arrival of the monsoon. The beach is tranquil except at weekends when it becomes a venue for bus tours.

Sorting nets at Benaulim

Continue 2km (1¼ miles) south to **Varca** fishing village. This has a mainly Christian community with their local chapel, **Nossa Senora da Gloria** (built in 1700), situated at the turn-off for the village. The beach here is even more peaceful than at Benaulim, although whispering causarina trees instead of swaying palms form the backdrop. To the south a couple of up-market resorts have developed. **Fatrade Beach** is pristine with soft white sands that stretch south rounding the mouth of the Sal River estuary past **Cavelossim**, 11km (7 miles) south of Colva, and **Mobor**, 2km (1¼ miles) beyond, a former fishing village where huge resorts loom on the horizon. The road ends here at a bus stop and one can hike to the tip of the peninsula at secluded **Betul Beach**.

Assolna school

Cabo de Rama fort

Back on the road, from the picturesque village square at Cavelossim, take the ferry across to **Assolna** village from where a pleasant country road leads towards ★ **Betul** village in Quepim *taluka*. This fishing village has a colourful jetty lined with dozens of boats and may be a good place to negotiate a boat ride up the Sal River and around its tiny islands with off-duty fishermen eager for some extra cash.

The road continues south across a varied landscape of tropical fruit trees, land reclamation plots and finally crosses some beautiful countryside through cashew plantations with scenic views until the turn-off for an unforgettable sight – the ruined fort at ★★ **Cabo de Rama** guarding the rocky bluff that juts into the sea. Named after the hero of the epic *Ramayana*, this spot is considered to be one of the sacred places where he lived during his exile. Of Hindu origin, the fort was taken by the Portuguese in 1763 and used as a prison until 1955. Solid outer ramparts, battered battlements and ruined turrets with a couple of old cannons still look threatening. Also there is a simple chapel and a government observation post. Behind the fort a path leads onto the tip of the promontory where there are dizzying 360-degree **views** of the ocean and the beaches.

Back at the crossroads, take the scenic route for 14km (9 miles) southwards to **Agonda**, a fishing village with a dramatic setting, silhouetted against three wooded hills. While strong undertows make swimming from the centre of the beach hazardous at certain times in the tide, bathing is safe at the rocky cove to the far south of the vast bay.

★★ **Palolem beach**, further south, has an idyllic setting: coconut palms sway overhead as a soft white sand is lapped by a gentle sea. From here, one can swim or wade over at low tide to minuscule **Canacona Island**, or take a dolphin-spotting trip for a couple of hours at sea to

Sunset at Palolem Bay

seek out these sleek swimming clowns. The bay is deservedly famous for its sunsets, although in recent years its essential tranquillity has been marred by the huge crowds of backpackers who descend here in the season. Most stay in one or other of the palm leaf 'hut' encampments lining the length of the beach, buildings in concrete having been wisely banned by the local municipality.

Walk across the rocks at the southern end of the bay to reach **Colomb** beach and fishing village and the deserted beach of **Patnem**. Beyond there it is possible to reach **Rajbagh** beach by boat or by wading across at low tide. A luxury resort was recently completed here, altering the atmosphere considerably.

Rajbagh boat service

The most secluded of these beaches, **Talpona**, is just across the river. **Galjibag**, backed by causarina plantations, is nearly always deserted, although its pristine sand supports Goa's largest population of Olive Ridley marine turtles, who nest here each winter. The eggs are protected by wardens who sleep by the nests to deter thieves.

From **Palolem**, head inland via Chaudi (2km/1¼ miles) on National Highway 17 where the crossroads are a transport hub for buses. Follow National Highway 14 and, at the signposted turn-off, go 7km (4 miles) northeast to reach the 16th-century **Mallikarjun Temple**. It is one of Goa's oldest Shiva temples despite its modern-looking exterior. Inside, in the main *mandapa* hallway, it has some very finely carved pillars. The temple celebrates a 'chariot' festival in February when the deities are paraded around on wooden chariots *(rathas)*, and there are all-night stage-performances of religious epics. The Shigmo Festival (end February/March) draws mass processions of pilgrims.

Mallikarjun Temple   **61**

Head south 7km (4 miles) to Goa's second largest nature reserve, the ★ **Cotigao Wildlife Sanctuary** (open from 8am, best season October to March). More than 105 sq km (40 sq miles) of densely forested woodland, washed by the River Talpona, rises into low hills. The park is a birdwatchers' delight, but lately there have been few sightings of any exotic animals. Wild boar, deer, gaur and monkeys abound, along with rare birds: the rufous woodpecker, the Malabar crested lark and the white-eyed eagle.

The park is also home to the **Kunbi** and **Velip** tribes who are subsistence farmers and are allowed to eke out a living by growing red chillies and harvesting the cashews within the precincts for sale in nearby towns. At the main entrance is the Forest Warden's Office and the Nature Interpretation Centre. The Forest Officer can arrange jeep trips within the sanctuary or a guide to the watchtower and waterholes from where one can observe animals feeding at dawn or dusk. Accommodation here is limited with just a few basic tents beside the Forest Rest House, which require advance written permission for occupation from the

Sacred banyan tree

DC Forests Office at Panjim (tel: 0832/225926). Alternatively, you can stay on a nearby spice plantation called Pepper Valley (tel: 264 2370), where a row of simple huts line a riverbank, shaded by areca palms.

On the return trip to the coast, stop off at **Partagali Village and Math** by the River Kushavati, a centre of religious education 6km (4 miles) southwest of Chaudi. The Math foundation is led by a Vaishnavite sect formed in 1475 at Margao, but established here much later. It offers a timeless setting for lessons near a ★ **sacred banyan tree**. The tree has a multitude of trunks and covers an area of 65m by 70m (213ft by 230ft), an enormous outdoor lecture hall. Priests recount how this banyan has existed for a thousand years and, like Hinduism, constantly regenerates.

After the crossroads at Chaudi, long golden beaches and wide river estuaries make for a very scenic drive. ★ **Polem**, 30km (18 miles) south of Chaudi, is Goa's southernmost beach, and is particularly tranquil, visited more by dolphins and sea eagles than tourists. It is located just 2 km (1¼ miles) before the Karnataka border at the submarine base of **Karwar**. Ask at Milan Bar & Café for directions.

Both Polem and Karwar were once centres of trade with Arabia and Zanzibar. These links are visible in the significant Muslim population still living along the coast.

Detour into Karnataka

From Karwar you can continue south along the spectacular coastline of northern Karnataka bordered by the jungly foothills of the Western Ghats. **Gokarna**, the seaside town that straddles two states, is a traditional centre for Hindu pilgrims devoted to Shiva and is riddled with shrines, temples and tanks. The place name is an amalgam of Goa and Karnataka. Pilgrims usually head for the beach to take their ritual bathe before offering prayers. Most popular are the medieval **Shri Mahabaleshwar Temple** at the western end of the bazaar and nearby Shri Mahaganpathi Temple.

South, beyond the laterite headland that overlooks the town, lie some superb beaches which make a good trek if one follows the trail from opposite the south gate of the **Mahaganpathi Temple**. Go down a narrow alley and head uphill for approximately 20 minutes. This eventually leads past **Kootlee Beach**, a long white sandy beach well below the path with a few *chai* stalls and cafés.

Om Beach

Or continue on for 40 minutes to ★★ **Om Beach**, a beautiful double crescent bay which seems to form the Om sign on the shore and attracts plenty of Western travellers. Intrepid beachcombers can go further south by a steep, rough path that leads to **Half Moon** and **Paradise** beaches. Fishing boats also ferry tourists out to these remote coves, which are served by a few simple cafés and hut camps.

Excursion to Hampi

Hampi, the ancient ruins of Vijayanagar

At ★★★ **Hampi**, an eight-hour train ride inland from Goa, are the fabled ruins of Vijayanagar, the lost capital of one of India's largest empires. Hampi is an awesome ghost city with finely carved temples and palaces all set in a landscape strewn with huge boulders. It ranks as a World Heritage Site and its ambience draws young backpackers who seek out the sacred 'power spots' said to exist here. Hampi is also believed to be the site of the mythical kingdom of Kishkindha, from the Sanskrit epic *Ramayana*. It was a kingdom of monkeys, whose ambassador Hanuman is a popular Hindu deity.

63

The easiest way to reach Hampi from Goa is to catch the twice-weekly train that runs from Margao (in the south of the state; see p 55) to the rail hub town of Hospet in Karnataka. The journey, which takes around eight hours, is a spectacular one, crossing the purple-covered Western Ghat mountains before beginning the long haul across the volcanic farmland of the Deccan plateau, with its endless cotton fields and boulder hills. From Hospet, local transport – in the form of taxis, buses and auto rickshaws – is on hand for the final half-hour, 13-km (9-mile) leg to the ruins at Hampi, where you'll find basic guest house accommodation. More comfortable hotels are available in Hospet.

On the road to Hampi

History

The powerful Vijayanagar kingdom was founded by two brothers from Andhra Pradesh – Harihara and Bukka, sworn enemies of the Kakatiyas. Later, they aligned themselves with the Muslim rulers of the Deccan, even converting to Islam. But eventually they became protégés of the Hindu sage Vidyaranya and went on to found a

Watering hole

Pilgrims bathing in the Tungabhadra River

Hindu kingdom, whose capital was established at Hampi in 1336. The empire rose to its peak under the great monarch Krishnadeva Raya (1509–29), a clever general and able adminstrator under whom trade with other kingdoms and countries flourished. During its golden age, this kingdom was legendary for its wealth and sophistication. Its multi-racial population included Jews and Parsis.

The Vijayanagar rulers were patrons and promoters of the arts and culture. They were also interested in developing new techniques in agriculture, warfare, water-works and civic building. More than 100,000 dwellings were erected. Craftsmen and merchants' guilds played an important role in the economic system. The bazaars overflowed with flowers and precious stones and trade with Burma, China, Arabia and Portugal flourished.

Although it was basically a Hindu kingdom, the rulers permitted the practice of other religions and they themselves followed a variety of Hindu cults – that of Virupaksha, Krishna, Vitthala, Rama and Venkateshwara. The Portuguese adventurer Paes, who visited Hampi in its heyday, described it as being as immense as Rome with palaces that dwarfed the ones at Lisbon.

However, by 1565 the Muslim Sultans managed to defeat the Vijayanagar army and the city was abandoned by the king and his court. Islamic armies sacked and plundered, until everything was utterly destroyed.

Today, this ruined city is perhaps the most beautiful and evocative of all the ruins in Karnataka. There is a brooding, mystical ambience in the landscape, whose desolation is offset by the magnificent remnants of this once powerful empire: ruined temples, palaces, bazaars and shrines.

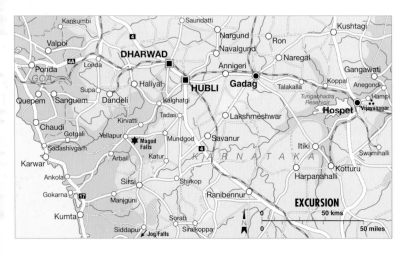

Sights

Vitthala Temple

The natural setting of the capital, with rocky ridges on three sides and the **River Tungabhadra** on the fourth, offered protection against invaders. The river flows through a rocky gorge which dominates the north, and extensive plains stretch towards the Sandur hills to the southwest.

On the south bank of the Tungabhadra, the main temples are located on rocky outcrops overlooking the ravine. This is the sacred axis of the city, believed to have existed before the founding of the kingdom. The rest of the city and its inhabitants seem to have lived in a 'dormitory town' across an irrigated valley.

Enter the lost city from the west, towards the sacred centre with **Hemkuta Hill**, where the 9th and 10th-century granite temples predate the Vijayanagar empire. They stand in clusters of two or three, built in an unembellished style with towers in the shape of stepped pyramids and terraces with gallery seating. Two granite monoliths carved with images of Ganesh also stand on this hill, as does a **Narasimha statue** carved out of a single boulder.

Virupaksha Temple

To the north lies the ancient ★★ **Virupaksha Temple** dedicated to this aspect of Shiva and his consort Pampa, a goddess symbolising the River Tungabhadra. Each year, at a festival attended by thousands of pilgrims, the **wedding of the god and his consort** is celebrated here. The two courtyards inside can be entered through gateway towers that loom 50m (160ft) overhead. The pillared hall leading to the main sanctuary has finely detailed carvings of animals and the ceiling is painted with legends of Shiva. It has a nine-storey high *gopuram*.

Outside to the east are the remains of the ancient ★ **Hampi Bazaar** whose colonnaded buildings still provide shelter to pilgrims and migrant labourers. Climb

Audience Hall

up **Matanga Hill** for a panoramic view of the city. The temple here is dedicated to a savage aspect of Shiva.

A short hike starts from the north gate of the Virupaksha Temple down to the **Sacred Ford** in the river. The original steps leading to the water are now abandoned since the river has changed course over the years. However, the traditional, basket-like **round boats** called *puttis* (coracles) are used to ferry villagers and tourists to the river bank on the other side where there is a handful of cafés and guest houses.

Another pleasant walk, about 1.5km (1 mile), along the river bank to the Vitthala Temple, passes several small shrines. Go through Achyuta Bazaar, past Tiruvengalanatha Temple and by **Sugriva's Cave** where, according to legend, the jewels of Sita, Rama's consort, which had dropped off during her abduction by Ravana were hidden by Sugriva. To the east one can see an ancient, ruined bridge. Continue past a 4th-century Narasimha Temple until the curious **King's Balance** near the entrance to the Vitthala Temple. Here, the kings were weighed against gold, jewels and grain that was later distributed among the poor, usually on the ruler's birthday.

Vitthala detail and sun chariot

Set in a walled courtyard, the 16th-century ★★ **Vitthala Temple** (open 8am–6pm; admisson fee) is dedicated to Vishnu. Built on a low elevation, the buildings form an elegant pattern, while the main tower is made of brick and plaster. The front hall has superb carvings of rearing animals and the detached columns are carved out of a single slab of granite. The ceiling is covered with carved floral and geometric motifs.

Vitthala visitors

To the east is the famed ★ **stone chariot** of Hampi, styled as a miniature shrine. Nearby is another ceremonial, pillared hall with intricate sculptures. Return via the

road, stopping at the hilltop **Raghunatha Temple** (great sunset views) or continue to the open-air **Queen's Bath**, 15m x 2m (49ft x 6ft), once filled to the brim with scented water from lotus-shaped fountains that were fed by the narrow moat around the bath.

Further up the road is the Durbar Enclosure where the royal family watched the Navaratri festival from a special platform, the **Mahanavami Dibba**, with fine carvings depicting scenes from battles, hunts and court entertainment. At the Royal Enclosure beyond there is a two-storeyed **Lotus Mahal**, said to be a true representation of the architectural style of Vijayanagar within the Zenana (women's quarters). To the east, a row of 10 chambers with high vaulted entrances centred around a two-storeyed pavilion that once formed the **Elephant Stables**.

Royal Enclosure: Lotus Mahal and watchtower

The small **Hazara Rama Temple** (1,000 Ramas Temple) features detailed friezes depicting scenes from the *Ramayana*. Proceed past the **Prasanna Virupaksha Temple** (also called the Underground Temple because it was buried beneath rubble at the time of Hampi's fall) to the Royal Residence Compound where there are Islamic-style gazebos and watchtowers.

67

The walled **Krishna Temple** dates from 1513 and has some fine carvings and shrines. The field across the road was once a 50-m (164-ft) wide path for religious processions. It is still marked by stray colonnades along the sides which were once part of a market area. Nearby, to the southwest, is a gigantic monolithic ★ **statue** depicting the half-man and half-lion form of **Lakshmi Narasimha** protected by the seven-headed serpent, Ananta.

Krishna Temple detail

Although many travellers are content to take in most of these sites within two days, it can be rewarding to stay in the area longer and take an excursion to the ancient fortress town of **Anegondi**. This trip can be made on foot or by bicycle – ideally by crossing the river on a *putti* from the ford near the Vitthala Temple or from the Sacred Ford below the Virupaksha Temple. Either way, it makes a 5-km (3-mile) loop through Anegondi, past a sacred bathing tank – Pampla Sarovar – and temple. Climb uphill to the small Hanuman Temple overloooking the north bank of the river for panoramic views of Hampi.

The route goes west towards an old stone bridge and across an island in the river. At Anegondi, a peaceful village thrives among scattered ruins, shrines and temples such as the **Huchchappa Mata Temple** near the river. It has remarkable black stone pillars and carved panels. In the centre, the Ranganatha Temple is still in use and in the village square there is a giant wooden temple **chariot**. There is a ruined palace called Aramani, once the home of the local nobility whose descendents still live opposite.

Art and Architecture

Whether a sherbet-hued Hindu temple with a domed pagoda, an austere fort barely discernible from the surrounding cliffs, or a village-size model of a Zanzibar palace, Goan architecture is eccentric. Even the proportions of simple white chapels can seem surreal, set against crooked coconut palms that bend double to thrash the windows, or with an oversize bell clanging away in an off-centre arch. Most old buildings in Goa seem imbued with a wistful other-worldliness. They show off a palimpsest of displaced styles, all reassembled in a bright tropical garden.

Lone survivor of conquests: Tambdi Surla Temple

From Goa's earliest days, conquerors would loot and pillage, then finally demolish most edifices right down to the foundations, only to re-fashion the rubble with an attempt at new grandeur. Gomant, Govapuri, Sandapur, Goa Velha, Ela: the same stones were recycled repeatedly. Elsewhere, believers whose gods were reviled by the current overlords would dismantle sacred altars with haste and stealth, safeguarding them with other treasures in some distant cache.

69

Sacred structures

Basilica of Bom Jesus

Wealthy traders and clerics could afford to pick and mix. Few were content simply to transplant architectural notions from Europe or the Orient for their domestic chapels and grander places of public worship. If materials were imported, delays were inevitable and the design plans could change whimsically in mid-construction. Almost all the surviving architectural treasures of Goa blend a range of symbols and styles.

Stark Buddhist caves close to the Arvalam waterfall were chiselled from an outcrop of rough laterite stone as early as the 4th century. A rounded hollow was scooped from each of the simple altar blocks which once held images of the Buddha, and an upright stone phallus set on every one. Shiva worship, represented by the basic *yoni* and *lingam*, displaced Buddhist rites here centuries ago.

Shri Saptakoteshwar Temple in Naroa

St Cajetan, or the Church of Divine Providence, stands in an Old Goa convent, but was built by Italian priests who were granted land in Goa by the Portuguese king after being banned from making conversions in distant Golconda. It is a 17th-century Goan baroque interpretation of St Peter's in Rome, with squared-off towers, a barrel vault, plus a free-standing altar piece. Wooden carvings by skilled Indian craftsmen curve with fecund promise. Surprisingly, right beneath the dome is an interior well hidden under a slab. Archaeologists suspect it is a portion of the main tank from a Saptakoteshwar Temple, demolished by zealous Portuguese fathers who outlawed worship of this powerful incarnation of Shiva.

Goa's Hindu temples, many rebuilt from scratch after the Inquisition ended, freely borrow arches and domes from Islam. Most feature an unusual tall lamptower called a *deepastambha*; when lit up, it becomes a column of flames offered to the deity. These pillars of light came to prominence during the Maratha Wars against the Moghuls and are unique to Goa. Scholars speculate that they could represent transformed and enlightened minarets, as the Marathas battled so fiercely against the Muslims.

What started out as a simple *stela*, with crevices for lamp oil and wicks, evolved in Portuguese baroque style. Soon the octagonal towers grew taller than the main sanctum, with glass windows all around for lamps. Many are painted with the same oyster-shell limewash used on so many churches for protection from monsoon humidity.

Cavelossim church

The tropics required specific adaptations in Portuguese church design. Windows were made slightly smaller to let in less heat, and they were set deeper into thick walls to help to protect the ornate gilded woodwork of the interior from excess damp and direct sunlight.

But such influences ran two ways. One of Goa's oldest unrefurbished chapels, built on the spot where Alfonso de Albuquerque commanded his 1510 battle against Adil Shah, is the Church of Our Lady of the Rosary. It resembles a fortress, with strong silo-shaped towers and moulding carved like twisted rope. This Manueline architectural detail (named after Portugal's King Manuel I, who reigned until 1521) is rare in Goa, where baroque church carving was trendier. Maritime themes – such as anchors, chains, ropes and sea creatures alongside tropical vines and exotic fruits – are typical motifs of the Manueline period and very distinct from earlier Moorish/Mudejar carving that avoided any naturalistic forms. Academics trace this ornate and very un-European style back to contact with Indian artisans, because it arose just as the first Portuguese explorers returned from India. Portuguese colonialists simply brought it back to its original source.

Portuguese legacy in domestic art

Elite Goans, who grew rich through trade with other Portuguese enclaves, quickly latched on to Iberian status symbols and many still persist. Decorative fountains, long familiar in Islamic courtyards, became more flamboyant with the use of ceramic tiles. Called *azulejos*, after their typical azure glaze, these blue and white tiles were highly valued for their durability (after installation), as well as for design possibilities. In Portugal, tiles were frequently incorporated into church decoration, but in Goa they were usually reserved for niches and benches in homes or shops. The best example in Goa is a large maritime mural on the wall at the Braganza Institute in Panaji.

Azulejos in Panjim

Very few *azulejos* were actually fired in India. Most of the fragile tiles were shipped to Goa from Macao, the Portuguese island off China, where quality was unsurpassed. This was also the source for porcelain vases and platters which decorate many traditional villas, though most pieces with polychrome glazes came from mainland China. The basic terracotta cookware turned out by Goan potters is more Indian than Portuguese.

Menezes-Braganza House in Chandor

Ornately carved Goan furniture is fashioned from rosewood or teak. Prized pieces are probably antique, especially if the finish is a flat ebony stain or cut-glass knobs are added. Woodworking and cabinetry hark back to the great trading epoch when termite-proof hardwoods came on galleons from Brazil or the West Indies and were crafted as future family heirlooms for the European gentry. Goan artisans proved to be wizards at intricate carving, never stinting on filling all available space. Apart from storage chests and a few low settees or platform tables, this furniture was primarily for colonial needs. Lovely four-poster beds and planter chairs can still be commissioned.

Antiques in Anjuna

The best setting for a suite of such furniture is the formal salon in a manor house, where it can be positioned symmetrically on burnished floorboards. Stately homes are rarely over two storeys high and usually face onto a central courtyard, just as an ordinary Goan house does. A verandah, open to the breeze, stretches along one entire side. Curved wrought-iron balconies jut out above it, and a two-tiered roofline accentuates the classic construction details. Old-fashioned homes may still have window panes of nacre, translucent 'oyster' shells which filter out the harsh sunlight. More typical Goan households feature a *balcao*, a wide-roofed porch supported by columns, that extends around two sides of the house exterior and provides plenty of shelter from sun or rain. Built-in benches encourage lingering for long gossip sessions.

Carnaval in Panaji

Cobra at the Nagpanchami

Folk Festivals and Music

Goans need no excuse for revelry, but by drawing on festivals from three separate religious traditions, they ensure plenty of celebrations throughout the year.

Hedonistic **New Year's** beach parties along the coast attract merry-makers from every Indian metropolis and from way beyond. For the **Feast of the Three Kings**, every 6 January, a trio of boys re-enacts the wise men's homage to the Christ Child. Naturally there is a big fête at Reis Magos, named after the holiday, but exciting events also take place at Chandor and Cansaulim.

Shivaratri, the February night when Lord Shiva destroyed the world with a celestial dance, requires powerful devotional hymns and fasting at Shiroda, Mangesh and Quela temples, among others.

Carnaval is hyped by the tourist board as a four-day mini-Rio, but is far lower-key and more covered up. King Momo teases masked dancers to stop traffic and follow him through the streets on floats. Also in late February, village women gather to sing lively *fugdis* and *dhalos* in the plazas for up to seven nights running, sometimes falling into trance. Holi, or **Shigmotsav**, features water fights and dabs of colour, plus drumming and cymbal-clashing.

Holy Week processions through the cobbled streets of Old Goa on Easter Monday are a compelling spectacle. The Sirigaum Temple to goddess Lairaya is mobbed on the first day of the **Hindu New Year**, with ritual coal-walking and flame-eating by devotees. Christians in Mapusa pay homage to Our Lady of Miracles on the same April day. In steamy summer, saints' days featuring songs that beg **St Anthony** for rain on 13 June or give rowdy toasts to **Sao Joao** for opening up the heavens on 24 June all are part of the monsoon cycle. At Calangute, boys jump into wells. Five days later, **St Peter** is honoured with a floating procession downriver near Fort Aguada. Three villages lash their best boats together to form a stage. During **Nagpanchami** in high summer, Hindus offer cobras bowls of milk and worship the thousand-headed snake.

Mass bathing off Divar Island on **Lord Krishna's birthday** (Janmashtami) commemorates his famous dip with 200,000 giggling milkmaids. On 24 August is the **Harvest Festival of Novidade**: after a mock battle between costumed conquistadors and Adil Shah's troops on the lawn of the Governor's Palace, the season's first rice is blessed and placed in the Novidade Cathedral. Idols of Ganesh, the elephant-headed Hindu god of auspicious beginnings, are set to sink in ponds, rivers, or the sea during a five-day post-harvest *festa* culminating in **Ganpati Chaturthi**. Brass bands and rockets add to the excitement.

Dussera (September/October) features bonfires and productions of the *Ramayana* epic. The Hindu festival of lights, **Diwali** (October/November), is like Christmas Eve and Guy Fawkes in one, and special sweets are offered. Once every decade, millions witness the relics of Goa's patron saint **St Francis Xavier** going from the Basilica and Se Cathedral in Old Goa on 3 December, the anniversary of his death, hoping for a new miracle *(see page 25)*. Martial marches mark **Liberation Day**, 17 December, when the Portuguese left Goa. After Midnight Mass at **Christmas**, families of all religions feast on goodies.

Diwali lights

Bom Jesus procession

Weddings, always checked by astrologers to ensure that the stars are auspicious, are a time to rejoice. Outsiders are often welcome to join in the fun, which includes hours of music and dance. **Zoitis** are folk tunes for each stage of the marriage. **Mando**, a traditional line dance where women flirt with fans while men flash handkerchiefs, is as mannered as a minuet and the romantic lyrics date back to 1920 or earlier. The **dekkni** is for women only, allowing prospective husbands to assess their grace, but the **dulpod** lets couples quick-step together. The older crowd may insist on hearing **fado**, a melodramatic Portuguese blues.

Listen out for **Remo Fernandes**. His fusion of Latin rhythms and Indo-rock with satire has won pop idol status. Live bands love to perform his hits, particularly from his first album, *Goan Crazy*. **Lata Mangeshkar**, with 30,000 Hindi film songs, is another icon. But after a slight at her home town temple in Ponda, she boycotts Goa completely. Still, her soundtracks are played everywhere and are very popular with Goans. The other great diva is Lorna, whose romantic, nostalgic songs have warmed the hearts of expatriate Goans separated from their families in the Gulf and beyond since the 1950s. You can pick up CDs at any market, or at CD shops in Panaji, Mapusa and Margao.

Food and Drink

Fresh seafood, whether deep-fried, grilled, or curried, is widely available. Locals go for mackerel, sardines, kingfish, shark steaks, crab, tiger shrimp, squid, ray or mussels. Some diners may prefer spicy sauces on the side. **Rechado**, a red, spicy sauce with *masala* (spice and chilli), is often doused over whole fish. **Kishmaur**, coconut, dried ground shrimp and chopped onion, is a favourite condiment. **Pilau** rice dishes are quite tasty and the seafood version is like paella without the olive oil. **Balchao**, an onion-based pepper sauce, normally comes with bread. Besides *chapattis* and *puris*, try the Goan **pao** (doughy inside), the crusty round **undo**, or hard-baked **polee** rings, best dunked in tea. **Sannan**, fermented rice pancakes with coconut, taste like South Indian *idlis*. **Red rice** gives a nutty flavour.

Fish for lunch

75

Sorpotel is strictly for carnivores: pig's liver and heart is pickled in sour tamarind and vinegar. **Leitao**, tender suckling pig, is better than the pork **vindaloo** in a marinade of wine vinegar, garlic and chilli. Spicy **chourico** sausage is fatty but flavourful, often served with **feijao**, haricot beans. **Chicken xacutti** is piquant with black pepper, star anise and coconut. **Cafrial**, peasant-style braised beef or mutton, is slow-cooked with garlic and pepper. Northern-style **tandoori kebabs** or **panir** cheese made from buffalo milk are popular and served in many cafés. Chinese, Thai, Italian, Tibetan, Israeli, and Afghan fastfood joints have sprung up.

Crème caramel or fruits make the best dessert: mango, papaya, custard apple and local bananas are good; giant jackfruit are oddly chewy. Sweets can be cloying: **bebinca**, a 10-layer coconut cake of egg yolks, nutmeg, ghee and raw brown sugar is as addictive as it is caloric. **Doce**, nutty fudge made with condensed milk, or **dodol**, semolina pudding with jaggery and coconut, are a bit lighter. **Alebele**, a fresh coconut pancake, is better for breakfast. **Bolinhas**, semolina cakes, are good for snacking anytime.

Curry and rice Molem

Often the food is best in expensive hotels. They often have all-you-can-eat buffets for a set price. **Penthouse Beach Resort** and the **Silver Sands Hotel** are high-class hotels with live bands playing most nights.

Alchohol is cheap in Goa. Chilled Kingfisher or San Miguel **lager**, bubbly local **vinho espumosa** and Riviera wine – drinkable whites and rosés from Maharashtra – are sold at most cafés, where you'll also find IMFL (**Indian made foreign liquor**). The rum and whisky, at least when mixed, are far better than local gin or vodka. Local **port**, palm toddy, and the potent **feni** (from the Konkan word *fen*, 'to froth') loosen up most of Goa's social life. Rarely exported because the locals drink the available supply, feni can be brewed from cashew nuts or coconut palm sap. It is similar to **arrack**, but has a smoother finish after a second fermentation.

Cashew feni

Refreshment at hand

Reliable **bottled water** is on sale everywhere, particularly Bisleri, but do check to see that the seal is intact. Unpurified water from the tap or well-water can cause dysentery. **Fresh fruit juice**, hand-squeezed from melons or berries, or **lassi**, a yoghurt shake, can be ordered plain, sweetened or salted. If a drink seems diluted, check that the added water is pure. Avoid ice cubes. **Nimbu pani**, fresh lime with bubbly water, is a thirst-quencher. Or order fresh **coconut water** and drink it straight from the green nut, then have it hacked in two to scoop out the flesh or 'cream'. Bottled Pepsi and Coca Cola prove less popular than hyper-sweet local brands. Individual cartons of guava, mango or apple juice have extra sugar, but are cheap and convenient.

Restaurants

Agonda

Dercy's Homely Family restaurant on the beachfront where the portions are gigantic. Ignore the menu and go for whatever the host, Inacio, suggests.

Anjuna

Blue Tao Energy-boosting juices, brown breads, crunchy salads, tofu spreads and other macrobiotic delicacies. **Martha's** Top venue for breakfast: try their fresh fruit and curd bowls or hot waffles with chocolate sauce.

Arambol/Harmal-Asvem

Double Dutch Axel and Lucie started out a decade ago by baking sublime apple pie (now delivered to restaurants across the state), then expanded into this delightfully idiosyncratic café. The pie's as good as ever, and they also do main meals (go for the stuffed peppers or buffalo steak). **Fellini's** Old Goa hands claim this is by far the best Italian restaurant in Goa, and it gets crowded with backpackers for their legendary home-made pasta in vongole sauce and wood-fired pizzas. **La Plage** Cool beachside café run by a French couple. Floaty white cotton drapes catch the breeze straight off the sea, and the food is appropriately light and sublime.

Baga

Dining option at Baga Beach

Fiesta Goa's most glamorous restaurant, bang opposite Tito's, run by two former models from Mumbai. Stylish Mediterranean cuisine is their forte. **Citrus** Smart little vegetarian place on Tito's Lane where ex-animal rescuer Nichola Maddox has devised a temptingly original menu, using mostly local ingredients. **Britto's** No stay in Baga would be complete without a stop at its most famous old beach restaurant, located at the mouth of the creek. A great venue for a sundowner. **Cavala** This red-laterite hotel on the roadside has two restaurants: one opposite, with a pool and fancy cocktail bar, and here, where the half-Russian chef offers tasty stroganoff and Anglo-Indian faves from Calcutta.

Benaulim

Palmira's Nowhere else in the village can hold a candle

to this place as a breakfast venue: Palmira's curd is the best for miles. Try it loaded onto a bowl of tropical fruit salad. **Palm Grove** Multi-cuisine restaurant in the hotel of the same name, sheltered in gorgeous gardens, lit up at night. **Johncey's** Giant beach shack that does a roaring trade throughout the season. Benaulim is one of the best places for fresh seafood, and you will get top quality here. **Domnick's** A bonfire and live music provide added incentive to venture up the beach for supper on Tuesdays, when Domnick's often parties into the small hours.

Betalbatim

Martin's Corner Legendary restaurant that started out as a shack for cabbies servicing the nearby five-stars, but has since expanded into a huge place only their foreign punters can comfortably afford. Despite her success, Mrs Martin still oversees preparation of the masalas personally.

Calangute

A Reverie Among the classiest addresses in Goa, with designer decor and food to match. **Infanteria Pastelaria** This bakery, run by the Souza Lobo family, is the place to come for old-style Goan sweets and puddings such as *bebinca* and *dodol*, and a good selection of main courses and proper coffee. **Souza Lobo's** Renowned seafront restaurant that was a local favourite years before the hippy era; their fish is fresh off the boats each day. **Platain Leaf** Goa's top south Indian, on the first storey of a large laterite building in the main market area: their *idli-wada* breakfasts are superb.

Candolim

Oriental Authentic Thai cuisine prepared by master chef Chawee, while her hospitable German husband, Henry, takes care of front of house. Try their papaya salad. **Sea Shell Inn** A perennial favourite; down-to-earth food at down-to-earth prices. Slick service, huge portions and a warm welcome from the Gonsalves family. **Amigo's** Eccentric riverside eatery under the Nerul road bridge, five-minutes inland. Rustic surroundings and wonderful seafood: go for the dressed crab or red snapper. **Pete's** A hot contender for the title of 'best shack in Goa', thanks to their sumptuous salad menu and ultra-hygienic kitchen. Proprietress Shanu's menu is always innovative. **Sheetal** Creamy sauces are the hallmark of this fine north Indian restaurant, where typical Mughlai dishes are served in copper *karai* dishes with piping hot nans. **The Stone House** Great value seafood and beef steaks, dished up to a backdrop of relentless Blues music.

Chapora-Vagator

Bean Me Up Healthy wholefood place in a similar vein to Blue Tao in nearby Anjuna, with Thai-style tempeh in nutty sauces and banana-tofu whip among the highlights. **Le Bluebird** French restaurant in the woods behind Ozran Vagator beach, boasting backpacker-friendly prices. Their pepper steak in brandy sauce gets rave reviews.

Alfresco in Anjuna

77

Daily delivery

Flea market in progress

Ready for haggling

Lutolim

Fernando's Nostalgia Located on the Ponda–Margao road, just outside the village. You can sample the full gamut of real Goan food and drink here – from chicken xacuti to coconut feni – on a mural-clad terrace.

Mapusa-Saligao

Florentine's This phenomenally popular restaurant, midway between Calangute and Mmapusa, serves a full Goan menu, but nearly everyone comes for the melt-in-the-mouth chicken cafreal, made to a secret recipe. **FR Xavier's** Charming old market café in colonial style. Try their legendary prawn puffs or vegetable patties.

Margo

Banjara Upscale north Indian place, off the main square. Does the full range of curry-house staples – chicken tikka, rogan ghosht and murg makahwalla – all to perfection. **Longuinho's** Colonial-era café that's worth a pitstop for the old-world atmosphere, with paddle fans and draught King-fisher beer. Tuck into a plate of their flaky 'veg puffs' or Portuguese-style 'prawn rissoles'.

Morjim

Hard Rock Café No connection with the American chain. This one's a beach shack – the first to have been sited on the sand spit at the far south end of Morjim beach, and still the pick of the bunch. It's run by local lad Gilbert Fernandes, whose menu features rock fish from the village. **Britto's** Rough-and-ready family-run shack, set in a new bandstand-style structure behind the beach, where you can enjoy the last word in local cooking. Clams from the nearby river in coconut masala, pan-fried mussels in millet, and Chapora calamari are among Sarah Britto's specials.

Panaji

Delhi Durbar Top-notch Mughlai cuisine that's rich, creamy and spicy, served in air-con comfort by white-turbaned waiters. Rogan ghosht (lamb) is their signature dish. **Shiv Sagar** The best of Panaji's many south Indian joints, serving crunchy masala dosas, as well as a host of regional, Chinese and Continental specialities (including spicy pizza). Be sure to order one of their wonderful fresh fruit juices. **Viva Goa!** Cheerful terrace restaurant tucked away in the heart of Goa's most picturesque quarter. Traditional Goan seafood dishes dominate the menu, from firey shark amotik to milder kingfish or mackerel in garlic butter.

Palolem-Patnem

Magic Italian The Italian owner of this busy restaurant on the beach road claims his pizzas, baked in a wood oven, are the best in India. His carbonara sauce is pretty fab too. **Oceanic Superb** Thai and north Indian curries are why people plod down the lane towards Colomb village to eat in this attractively set up restaurant, run by a British couple. Their tandoori specialities are great, but make sure you leave room for the lemon and ginger cheesecake. **Droopadi** Slap on the beach and the best place in Palolem proper for traditional Mughalai food. Murg makhini (chicken in a creamy spiced gravy) is the house speciality. **Cozy Nook** This is the place to head for if you're craving healthy salads, washed in iodised water, from an 'all-you-can-eat' buffet that's prepared fresh each day. **Home** Stylish Swiss-run beach café in Patnem, just south of Palolem, where you can enjoy sunny Mediterranean salads with real olive oil and perfect espresso.

Shacks

Goa's beaches are backed by palm-leaf cafés set up to cater for foreign tourists during the winter. In addition to chilled soft and alcoholic drinks, they also serve light snacks and meals of mainly seafood such as kingfish, pomfret, shark, tiger prawns and calamari, prepared with chips and salad garnish. Generally speaking, shack food is far cheaper than that served in hotels, which can be up to five times the price.

Propping up the bar

Shopping

Most shops near Goa's beaches offer a range of handicrafts, curios and jewellery from other regions of India. Basic swimwear is available, plus big scarves for beach wraps. Leatherware shops offer a choice of bags, sandals and other items. **Beach hawkers** selling Rajasthani clothes, scarves and jewellery are everywhere; make sure you haggle. The **flea market** held on Wednesdays at **Anjuna Beach** expands each year as vendors from Tibet, Kashmir, Rajasthan, Gujarat and other parts of India come for the season. A wide range of handicrafts, clothes, jewellery, beachwear and travel gear is available, and there are international food stalls. The **Saturday night** market near **Arpora** has interesting handmade jewellery, antique silver buckled belts, rave gear, bikinis and lycra tops from Bali, plus homemade cakes. It starts around 5pm during high season. Musicians and street artists perform here. To see all the colour of a **regional market**, with gadgets, produce and livestock as well as tourist trinkets, make the effort to go to **Mapusa** on Friday mornings.

Party time on the beach

At **Camelot** in Ribera, near **Old Goa**, home accessories and textiles are displayed alongside Indian couture. Look out for fashions by designers like Ritu Beri and Rohit Bal. Another "Lifestyle Emporium" worth a browse is **Salgondar**, a short way inland from Calangute, which showcases fine arts and crafts from around the country, along with beautiful antique or reproduction furniture. The building, a grandly restored Portuguese-era *palacio*, is worth a visit in itself. Next door, **Saudades** offers a similar range of goods in another period house. In Baga, **Casa de Goa** is a small boutique on the main road where you can buy Goan souvenirs: azulejos, paintings, books, objets d'art and clothes.

Nightlife and Entertainment

Nightlife in Goa tends to be tame by European standards – the coastal belt is densely populated with working families who resent noctural disturbance. Previously the state was famous for parties and raves, but these now take place rarely (the government restricted 'amplified music' in 1999).

Anjuna
Laguna Anjuna This funky designer hotel hosts regular pool-party nights, featuring international DJs: Goa Trance for the discerning and well-heeled. **Paradiso de Goa** Stacked up a slope behind a cove at the north end of Anjuna beach has a groovy dance floor surrounded by UV-reactive figures of Hindu deities. Popular mainly with young Israeli ravers.

Arambol/Harmal
Double Dutch Axel and Lucie's chilled café-restaurant is the venue for Indian Classical recitals (by teachers from Panaji's Kala Academy) each Sunday morning. **Loekie's** Twice weekly (Sunday and Thursday) jam sessions – of varying quality – with whoever happens to be in town. When this place is quiet, try the **Mango Tree** further up the lane.

Baga
Cuba Cubana Arpora's 'Nightclub in the Sky' is on a hilltop behind the coastal strip, with a hefty R&B/hip-hop/garage sound system, underlit pool; entry includes unlimited drinks. **Ingo's Night Bazaar** The original and best of the two night markets at Arpora, favoured by the alternative expat community, who sell designer tangas and fluoro party gear. A big stage hosts live bands, and food stalls serve international dishes. **Kamaki** Popular karaoke bar with widescreen sports TV and glacial air-con. Packed with young Brits. **Mambo's** Glorified beach shack with a kicking karaoke system that stays open until well after midnight, serving cocktails as well as draught beers. This is where the reps let off steam. **Tito's** Famous all over India, Tito's draws huge crowds (of mostly young Indian men) during the season, when its DJ nights are supplemented with occasional fashion shows and live acts. Their door policy favours women and penalises single men.

Benaulim
Domnick's Tuesday evening firework and bonfire nights roll into fun parties on a sandy dance floor – about as lively as Benaulim gets. **Pedro's** Frequent live music – by local cover bands of the kind that normally play cruise liners – add a bit of a buzz to weekends at the beachfront. Be there early.

Calangute–Candolim
Bob's Inn One of Goa's oldest bars, a hangover from hippy days where hard-drinking old freaks still congregate around a long wooden table. **Congo** Glamorous new open-air club-restaurant that's become the favourite watering hole of rich 30-somethings from Mumbai and Delhi. Thai appetisers and

sumptuous desserts tempt people out of the four-posters in the lounge; the music's ambient techno. **Kathakali Recital** At the roundabout on Calangute beach road, a first-storey theatre holds nightly recitals of Kerala's amazing ritual dance drama, Kathakali, complete with authentic costumes and make up. **Kerkar Art Gallery** Indian Classic music recitals take place in the garden of this little art gallery each Tuesday from 6.45pm, lit by pretty lanterns and candles. Details on-line at: www.subodhkerkar.com/auditorium.htm

Panjim

Kala Academy Panaji's cultural hub lays on frequent India music and dance recitals, as well as exhibitions by students, tutors and visiting artists. Check the local papers for details. **Innox** Goa's first and only multiplex cinema, screening all the current Bollywood blockbusters, plus occasional foreign language movies with subtitles.

Vagator-Chapora

Primrose Bar Full-on bar hidden in the woods in the village. Decked out with rave-y fluoro murals, it has a thumping trance sound system. This is where everyone comes after the Nine Bar shuts. **Nine Bar** Laterite-lined dance floor overlooking Ozran Vagator beach, with Goa's heftiest PA and a more mixed clientele than Paradiso. DJs queue up to play here. Best on Wednesdays after the flea market.

Candolim Beach

Active Pursuits

Clunky Hero **bicycles**, the standard Indian one-gear two-wheeler, are for hire in most main towns.

Parasailing sessions are held in high season on the stretch of beach between Calangute and Baga. Parasailers should weigh more than 6½ stone (41kg). Once the parachute is rigged up to a motor boat, you lift-off and touch-down right on the sand, but as the boat runs parallel to the shoreline, you soar high above the water. Experienced aides encourage and disentangle first-timers. Paragliding is quite different. Instructors guide students to a bluff between Baga and Anjuna beaches and to the cliffs dividing Arambol and Querim beaches, depending on the wind direction.

Top **watersports** facilities are found at most five-star resorts. The silty waters along the coast aren't all that great for sub-aqua pursuits, but one outfit – Goa Diving, at Bogmalo Beach – takes trips out to the islands off-shore, where visibility is considerably better. They also run longer trips down to Karnataka that take in a few excellent wreck sites. For more information go to www.goadiving.com

Treks in Goa's hinterland, keeping inland from the coast, feature in some package tours and are aimed at keen bird-watchers. You'll need sturdy shoes with ankle support and lots of mosquito repellent if exploring the Western Ghats.

Dudhsagar Falls, in the jungle

Getting There

Independent visitors to Goa must normally land in Delhi, Mumbai or Chennai, then either travel by rail or take an internal flight to Dabolim airport. Jet Airlines, Indian Airlines and Air Sahara have frequent scheduled flights to Goa from a dozen or more Indian cities. Direct charter flights from the UK, Germany or Scandinavian countries invariably include accommodation, and can rarely be extended. Yet taking advantage of the low-priced tickets can save savvy travellers a considerable amount of money. It is well worth surfing the Internet to search out options to suit your particular circumstances.

Indian citizens can't use charter flights to Goa as an entry point, to which end a restriction of four weeks is placed on stays by those arriving by charter. It is also forbidden to leave India by scheduled flight if you arrived on a charter. Long-staying visitors get around this problem by ditching the return half of their tickets and purchasing another one to travel home at the end of their stay in Goa. Flights on charter to the UK may be bought via Davidair in Candolim (tel: 0832 2489303; www.com2goa.com). Round-trip tickets are required on all charters. In the UK, Monarch Airlines (tel: 0870 405040, www.monarch-airlines.com) depart from Luton airport. There is also a weekly departure on Monarch from Manchester. These flights re-fuel in the Gulf en route, and take more than 11 hours to reach Dabolim airport. Bookings for the peak tourist season from December to January can increase the price of tickets considerably.

Via Mumbai: British Airways, tel: 0870 850 9850, and Air India, tel: 020 8560 9996, fly direct daily to Mumbai. Emirates, tel: 0870 243 2222, also flies via the Middle East as do Gulf Air, Kuwait Airways and Royal Jordanian.

From Mumbai: There are numerous flights between Mumbai's domestic airport, Chatrapathi Shuraji, and Dabolim airport, operated by: Indian Airlines, Air India, Sahara India Airlines and Jet Airways. The 1-hour flight costs around US$75–100.

Arrivals: Goa's Dabolim Airport is situated 30km (18½ miles) south of Panaji. It has limited facilities and getting through immigration can take up to an hour. A pre-pay taxi counter is situated immediately outside the arrivals hall, which clearly displays rates to all the main destinations . Buy a ticket, hold onto the receipt until you reach your destination, and don't let the taxi driver persuade you to go to another hotel (for which he will get a commission), whatever the excuse. Upon request many of the hotels can also arrange for an airport transfer.

Local air travel: Dabolim Airport, tel: 512788/513863/510917, is near Vasco da Gama, 30km (18 miles) south of

Travel agents in Panaji

Panaji. There are flights to many places in India – Bangalore (1½ hours, two daily), Chennai (two weekly), Delhi (two daily), Kochi (two weekly) and Mumbai (1 hour, ten daily). During the Christmas season flights may have to be reserved months in advance. To get a flight to Delhi or Mumbai from Goa during January, you will usually have to arrange it several days in advance.

The Chorao ferry

Train: Goa is connected with Bangalore, Delhi, Mysore, Pune and Hyderabad by rail, and Mumbai by the new Konkan Railway. There are about four trains a day from Mumbai to Goa, taking between 7 and 11 hours. You will need to reserve tickets well in advance. The UK agent for Indian Railways is SD Enterprises in Wembley, tel: 020 8903 3411. There are two trains on the spectacular Konkan Railway route that arrive in Goa daily from Mumbai (the Mandovi Express and Konkankanya Express, both from Mumbai CST). Tickets are sold at the railway stations in Margao and Vasco da Gama, and at the bus station in Panaji. See also www.konkanrailway.com If coming from the south of India/Kerala, there are direct trains from Thiruvananthapuram (Trivandrum): the Rajdhani Express takes 16 hours; the Netravatri Express takes 20 hours. Direct trains also run between Vasco da Gama and Delhi and Bangalore (15 hours), and from Mathura to Madgaon, in south-central Goa. The South Central Railway reservation counter is open daily (10am–1pm and 2.30–5pm) at the Panaji bus stand, upstairs in the main building. The tourist quota is limited. A local travel agency can reserve train tickets if given advance notice. For timetables, fares etc. visit: www.indianrailways.com or www.konkanrailway.com

Ready for the road

By coach

You can book Kadamba bus tickets in advance at Panaji and Mapusa bus stands (9–11am and 2–5pm). A night bus from Mumbai to Goa takes 15–18 hours. It is an uncomfortable 500-km (310-mile) trip on rough roads. The trip going south from Goa is easier. Private bus companies operate buses to Mumbai, Pune, Hampi, Bangalore and many other places. You can book buses to and from Goa from travel agencies.

Getting Around

White Maruti vans can be hailed or approached at parks near hotels and tourist sites. Fares should be fixed in advance with the driver: four passengers easily fit inside. Metered yellow-top taxis can be hired at a pre-paid counter at rail stations and the airport, and hailed in the big towns. A taxi can be rented for a day (8 hours) or a half-day (4 hours). Painted black and yellow like hornets, three-wheel scooters don't always use meters, and haggling may be necessary. Suspension is considerably better than the North Indian version. Licensed drivers must wear a khaki shirt. Another version of transport is for a passenger to sit behind a 'pilot' on a motorcycle with white plates. It is best to wear closed shoes and to agree on the fare at the outset. Rates are usually Rs5 per km.

Proximity to the sea coupled with numerous creeks and rivers criss-crossing the Goan hinterland, makes water transport one of the cheapest and most easily available modes of transport in Goa. For tourists, it has the added attraction of observing the countryside and glimpsing the Goan life. Regular launch and ferry services are the backbone of water transport. From sun-up to late evening, a fleet of flat-bottomed ferries cross Goa's rivers carrying pedestrians, cars, taxis and motorcycles on average three times an hour. These are often the only way of crossing the numerous waterways.

Rickshaw arrival

Trains leave from Vasco da Gama or Margao station. There are good connections to Hospet (for Hampi) *(see Route 4, page 38)*. Kadamba, the state-run company, and numerous private operators provide a cheap, comprehensive and frequent bus service, but journey times can be slow.

Car and jeep rentals are available, but you should have an international driving licence and it may be safer to rent a car with a driver since the difference in cost is minimal. Enquire at your hotel or at any tourist office. A popular, if highly dangerous, way to get around the state.

Facts for the Visitor

Entry
A valid tourist visa for a six-month period from the date of issue (not entry) costs £30. You need to specify whether you require a single-entry or a multiple-entry visa, but as they cost the same ask for the latter which is more flexible. Apply at the Indian consulate or High Commission in your country of origin. Visas are also available by post; allow at least a month for processing. Apart from an emergency, the only way to extend your visa is to leave for Nepal or Sri Lanka and apply for a new visa.

UK: Indian High Commission, India House, Aldwych, London WC2B 4NA, tel: 020 7632 3149; www.hcilondon.org

There are two customs channels: green for passengers carrying non-dutiable items and red for those with dutiable goods. Duty-free items include one litre each of wine and spirits, 200 cigarettes/50 cigars/250g tobacco and all personal belongings. See also www.customs.com

Timetable

KONKAN RAILWAY				
TIVIM STATION				
TRAIN TIMING				
DOWN TRAINS		UP TRAINS	
TRAIN No.	ARRIVAL	DEPARTURE	TRAIN No.	ARRIVAL	DEPARTURE
KHR 1	18.00	18.01	KHR 2	08.40	08.41
KR0111	09.12	09.14	KR0112	19.28	19.30
2616	20:30	20:32	2617	05:26	05:28
6337	07:06	07:08	6338	10:58	11:00

Tourist information
On the Internet: www.incredibleindia.org
In the UK: Indian Government Tourist Office, 7 Cork St, London W1X 2LN, tel: 020 7437 3677, fax: 020 7494 1048.

Patience is a virtue

When to go

October to March is the best time. The peak season is from mid-December to the end of January, when temperatures are around 32°C (90°F). Book well in advance for Christmas/New Year (party season), when: accommodation rates usually double. Monsoon season is June–mid-September when most of the beach shack cafés and bars are closed.

Currency and exchange

The Indian currency is called the Rupee (Rs.). There are 24-hour currency exchange counters at all international airports. Most banks offer at a better exchange rate than hotels, but this may involve a wait and big hotels offer 24-hour service. Travellers' cheques and most international credit cards are increasingly accepted, especially in the larger towns and establishments. US dollars are easiest to convert, with sterling a close second. Alternatively, you can withdraw Indian currency direct using your cash card at any of dozens of ATMs in Goa's towns and resorts. Nearly all of the major banks – notably UCI, ICICI and Andhra Bank – have ATMs; most remain open (and attended by a security guard) 24/7. Almost all money is paper, which can get in a terrible state. Don't accept torn banknotes as nobody (except major bank branches) will be prepared to accept them from you. Large denominations can be a problem in small towns and villages. Banking hours are Monday to Friday 10am–2pm, Saturday 10am–noon. However, private exchange companies in Panjim and the main coastal resorts are the best all-round places to change foreign notes and currencies.

Post

All small towns have post offices (10am–5pm, closed weekends) and the larger towns have General Post Offices (9.30am–5.30pm, closed Sunday). Mail takes an average of 10 days to get to its destination outside the country. Poste Restante services are available at most post offices. Parcels of up to 1m (3ft) length and weighing up to 20kg (44lb) can be sent by post, although it is a long and complicated process and it is better to check the local requirements first.

Internet and Email Services

Goa is well provided with Internet access points. You'll find 'cybercafés' in all the resorts and towns, increasingly with broadband as well as dial-up connections. Most charge by the half-hour. Hardware tends to be modern, using up-to-date software, although keyboards are frequently in poor shape. Travellers carrying their own laptops can plug these in; normal charges apply. If you do bring your own portable computer, it's worth investing in a UPS (current surge protecting device) to protect your hard drive if the place you'll be using it most frequently doesn't have one.

Helpful information

Telephone

Public telephone booths with International Direct Dialling and Subscriber Trunk Dialling facilities are widely available. Some also offer fax and e-mail services and they are far cheaper than hotel phones. Customers can confirm the number dialled and monitor expenses on the screen. Telephone numbers in Goa change constantly and the directories when available are often out of date.

To call abroad, dial the international code (00), the code for the country (44 for the UK), the area code (leaving out any initial zeros), and the number you want. The national code for Goa is 0832; when dialling internationally this is +91 832. Privately run phone offices with international direct dialling facilities are widespread. Calls are dialled direct and you pay the bill after the call. All major hotels and travel agencies, as well as most STD booths will send and receive faxes.

Cruise operator

Mobile Phones

You should be able to use your mobile phone handset in Goa to send and receive calls, although your home network provider will have to switch on your coverage in India. Note that charges are made for incoming calls and texts as well as outgoing ones when you're abroad. In an attempt to save money, lost of mobile phone users invest in an Indian SIM card while on holiday. These entitle you to use one of the local networks for periods of between seven and 30 days. However, you still have to pay for incoming calls and it's debatable whether switching actually works out cheaper. Of the Indian network providers, Ideal (formerly AT&T) is considered to have the best coverage in Goa.

Get your rupees here

Tipping

In large hotels, a minimum tip of 10 percent is expected and more is appreciated, but smaller places seem content with less. Bell boys expect around Rs10 per bag. Tourist guides, taxi drivers and porters have a minimum rate.

Health

Check with the embassy about current health requirements and get inoculated well in advance. Vaccinations against hepatitis A, typhoid and meningitis, tetanus and polio are recommended. Malaria exists in Goa. It is advisable to take precautions against mosquito bites, take anti-malarial medicine and always sleep under a good net without holes. (Bring one with you as those available locally aren't always top quality.) Tuberculosis is still present in India. Tap water is not safe to drink; always buy bottled water and check the seal is intact. Also, care should be taken when eating, as few Western travellers escape without a bout of diarrhoea. Avoid uncooked salad, chutneys and sauces, ice and peeled fruit, etc. Drink plenty of water and wear sunscreen and a hat in hot weather. Carry your own medicines if you have a chronic problem, although chemists are well stocked and large towns have 24-hour pharmacies. Pack DEET-based insect repellent to protect against mosquitoes and sandfleas.

Clothing
Take cotton clothing and be prepared to dress modestly – women should avoid sleeveless blouses and mini skirts. Nudity is illegal, including on the beaches, and wandering around town in beachwear is disapproved of and ignores local sensibilities. In winter, it can get fairly cold on the beach.

Connecting people

Crime
Increasing crime problems in Goa are linked with the tourist boom. Items left unattended on the beach, or in your room, may be stolen. If you have a ground floor room, be sure the windows are locked when you go out, as thieves often use a stick to fish things out through an unlocked window. Some hotels have safe deposit boxes in the family house of the people who own the hotel. If you have travellers' cheques, leave them and your passport with the family from whom you are renting. Because they are native to Goa, and because they rarely leave their houses unattended, they are less likely to be robbed.

Violent crime is not typical of Goa, but there are several cases where women have been attacked while alone on the beach. Lone women should be on their guard in secluded areas, especially at twilight or at night. Women should also be careful of the motorbike taxi drivers at night, especially if the driver has been drinking. Do not engage in small talk with them. There are known cases of such drivers attempting to rape Western women.

Emergencies
In case of an accident, get the injured person to hospital by taxi: ambulance services are often delayed and coastguard services are inadequate. Scanners are available at few places – Salgonkar Medical Research Centre (tel: 0832 512524) in Vasco da Gama has one. Goa Medical College Hospital at Bambolim (tel: 0832 222 5727) is the best in the state; there is also a branch in Panaji (tel: 0832 224566).
Police: 100
Fire Brigade: 101
Ambulance: 102

Diplomatic representation
Most countries have embassies and consulates in New Delhi. The UK maintains a Tourist Assistance Office in Goa: Ms Shilpa Caldeera, 13/14 Dempo Towers, Patto Plaza, Panaji (tel: 0832 243 8897, fax: 0832 564 1297; www.ukinindia.com)

Accommodation

The hotels and guest houses listed below are the better options. Prices vary considerably: **£** = up to £10 per night. **££** = up to £50 per night; **£££** = around £100 per night.

Agonda

Dercy's, tel: 264 7503. Recently built double-storey block of rooms facing the beach, with cheaper leaf huts opposite and a great little seafood restaurant on a ground-floor terrace. Impeccably clean and hospitable. **£**

Dunhill Beach Resort, tel: 264 7604. A short way up the lane from Dercy's, and the best fallback: little en-suite rooms opening on to a sandy yard. Again, well kept and there's a congenial café-restaurant serving fresh fish. **£**

Anjuna

Anjuna Beach Resort, De Mello Waddo, tel: 227 4499; email: fabjoe@sancharnet.in. Large rooms with balconies, refrigerators and hot water. A new block also has furnished flats, at competitive rates for the area. **£**. **Don Joao Resort**, Soronto Waddo, tel: 227 4325; www.goacom.com/hotels.donjoao. A large two-star that was designed for the package market but now accommodates mostly independent travellers. All rooms have balconies, bathrooms and fridges. **££**. **Granpa's Inn (Bougainvillea)**, Gaun Waddo, tel: 227 3270; www.goacom.com/hotels/granpas. One of the few places you can stay in an old Portuguese-era house, surrounded by lovely gardens, with a pool and modern amenities on site. **££**. **Laguna Anjuna**, De Mello Waddo, tel: 227 4305; www.lagunaanjuna.com. Chic boutique hotel comprising 25 stone roundel houses designed by famous Goan architect, Dean D'Cruz. There's a dreamy pool and the complex is screened by greenery. **££–£££**. **Lotus Inn**, tel: 227 4015; www.lotusinngoa.com. An off-beat, alternative resort hotel run by Goan-German couple, with all modern comforts (including a great pool), comfortably furnished chalets and a good restaurant, though it's a long walk from the beach. **££**. **Palacete Rodrigues**, near Oxford Stores, Mazal Waddo, tel: 227 3358; www.palaceterodrigues.com. Delightful colonial-era mansion, with deep verandah, hundreds of pot plants and rooms lovingly furnished with family heirlooms. **££**. **Palmasol Guest House**, behind St Anthony's church, tel: 227 3258. A good budget option if you want to be really close to the beach. The rooms in the old block are larger and more expensive than those in the modern annexe. **£**. **Peaceland**, Sorranto Waddo, tel: 227 3700. Set well back in the village, just off the main road in a well shaded compound, and one of the best budget guest houses in the area. Their rooms are nicely kitted out, with clothes racks, nets and chairs; all rooms en-suite with ground-floor verandahs. **£**. **Villa Anjuna**,

89

Help is at hand

beach road, tel: 227 3443 or 227 4239; www.anjunavilla.com. Smart, newish hotel close to the beachfront, popular with mostly young fun-lovers. The pool is the main attraction, but there's also a jacuzzi, internet access and all the facilities of a three-star (including optional a/c), at a fraction of the cost. **£–££**

Arambol

Ave Maria, House No.22 Modlo Waddo, tel: 229 7674; email: avemaria_goa@hotmail.com. This has long been the largest and most popular guest house in the village: simple, but clean, with or without en-suite bathrooms, and there's a sociable rooftop terrace. **£. Fanfama**, Kalcha Waddo, tel: 229 2516; www.travelingoa.com/famafa. Modern, comfortable accommodation very close to the beach in rooms with tiled floors, block-print bedspreads and balconies. It can be noisy in the evenings. **£. Ivon's Cottages**, Girkar Waddo, tel: 229 2672. Immaculately clean, secluded and altogether pleasant little guest house down in the fishing quarter, south of the village centre. The rooms are tiled, with bathrooms, and open on to large common balconies. Three minutes' walk to a quiet stretch of the beach. **£**

Aswem-Mandrem

Dunes, Junasa Waddo, Mandrem beach, tel: 224 7219/ 224 70701. Large encampment of leaf huts, each kitted out with their own twin beds, fans and tables. Slap on the beach, and with its own restaurant, but it can get crowded here in peak season. **£. Elsewhere**, Aswem-Mandrem, tel: 00 91 22/237 38757; http://aseascape.com. If you love traditional Goan architecture and deserted beaches, then you won't find anywhere more inspiring than this exclusive hideaway, on the last stretch of undeveloped sand in north Goa. Crowning a low dune, the 19th-century house has a breezy verandah, and sleeps six in luminous rooms. **£££. Villa River Cat**, Junasa Waddo, Mandrem, tel: 224 7928; www.villarivercat.com. Rinoo Seghal and his Finnish ex-wife created their dream guest house here, sandwiched between the dunes: a circular mansion filled with mosaics, devotional sculptures, romantic terraces, cats and dogs. The 16 rooms are gorgeous and there's a relaxing waterside garden. **££**

Baga

Alidia, Saunta Waddo, tel: 227 6835. Modest guest house on the dunes, right behind the beach, with large, well furnished rooms that are all en-suite and have balconies. **£. Andrade ('Rita's')**, off Tito's Lane, tel: 227 9087. Best of the budget places in this busy area, close to the nightlife and beach. Tidy, clean rooms, sea-facing balconies. **£. Divine**, tel: 227 9546; email: divinehome@satyam.net. Tucked away north of the river in a much quieter location than most. There are only four rooms here, centered on a cosy leafy courtyard, but they're lovingly kept and peaceful. **£.**

Budget accommodation in Panaji

Anjuna courtyard

Nilaya Hermitage, Arpora Bhati, tel: 227 6793/227 6794; www.nilayahermitage.com. On a hilltop overlooking the coastal belt, this chic 'boutique hotel' has the air of a millionaire's hideaway. Each room occupies a stone chalet individually styled in sunny colours, with designer fittings and furniture blending east and west, and the pool is a dream. **£££**.

Rohil Beach Resort, tel: 227 6101/227 6099; www.goacom.com/hotels/ronil. One of the better package-oriented hotels on the Baga strip, with a good-sized pool and architecture that makes an attempt to look Goan. All the facilities you'd expect from a 3-star, including 2 pools. **££**.

Vila Fatima, Baga Road, tel: 227 7418. Large guest house popular with young backpackers, behind the beach. **£**.

Benaulim

Anthy's, Sernabatim, tel: 277 1680; email: anthysguesthouse@rediffmail.com. Good-sized en-suite rooms with airy verandahs, slap on a beautiful bit of beach. The staff are friendly and the café-restaurant a great spot for sunset. **£. Camilson's**, Ambeaxir-Sernabatim tel: 277 1582; www.camilsons.com. The most appealing and friendly of a string of three 'resort' guest houses, north of Benaulim. Its rooms are pleasant and open on to a well-tended garden. Pricy for Benaulim – you pay for proximity to the surf. **£–££**.

Oshin Cottages, Mazil Waddo, tel: 227 0069. A dependable budget choice: dozens of rooms in a three-floored building overlooking paddy fields. A good walk (15mins) from the sea, but quiet. **£. Palm Grove Cottages**, Tamdi-Mati, tel: 277 0059/277 1170; www.palmgrovegoa.com. The nicest mid-range option, offering spacious tiled rooms, double or twin beds, hot water and views from the balconies through lush foliage towards the sea. Swathed in greenery, the restaurant makes the most of its garden location. **£–££. Succorina Cottages**, House No.1711/A, Vas Waddo, tel: 277 0365. A cosy little guest house, comprising half a dozen spotless en-suite rooms, the best of them with balconies looking across the fields to the sea. Hidden at the southern fringe of the village, in the appealingly ramshackle fishers' quarter, it's a 20-minute walk from the shops, but tranquil – and the rates are rock-bottom. **£. Tansy**, beach road, tel: 277 0574. Various sized 'apartments', from rooms with kitchenettes to fully furnished two-bedroom flats. All come with big bathrooms and fridges, and they're handy for the village centre. **£.**

Taj Exotica, south of Benaulim village, tel: 227 1234140. Flagship five-star resort of the famous Indian chain, boasting 140 centrally air-conditioned rooms in a grand complex fronting the beach. Facilities include a nine-hole golf course, health spa and world-class waterports kit. **£££**

Bogmalo

Bogmalo Beach Resort, Bogmalo, tel: 255 6222, fax: 255 6236. Ugly five-star in Costa mould whose (only) re-

91

Cooling off in Candolim

Fort Aguada Beach Resort

deeming feature is its stupendous view over the bay. **£££**. **Coconut Creek**, in UK tel: 0800 169 6841. This small resort hotel, hidden in a palm grove behind Bogmalo beach, has been universally acclaimed for its Goan-inspired architecture. The romantic rooms are ranged around a lagoon-shaped pool, and there's a classy restaurant. **£££**. **Joet's**, on the beach, tel: 253 8036. Congenial, welcoming family-run guest house right on the beach, with only half a dozen rooms (some of them air-conditioned). Most of its guests are returning customers. **£–££**

Calangute

Arabian Retreat, Gauro Waddo, tel: 227 9053; www.arabianretreat.com. Simba the cat and Foxy the dog are the big attractions at this homely guest house, shaded by areca palms on the edge of Calangute. The rooms are well furnished, with balconies on both sides, good-sized bathrooms and fridges. **££**. **Coco Banana**, 1195 Umta Waddo, tel: 227 6478; www.cocobananagoa.com. Swiss-Goan couple, Marina and Walter Lobo, have run this model guest house since the hippy era. It has large, attractively furnished rooms, with extra-long beds and nets, opening on to a secluded courtyard. **££**. **Gabriel's**, another old favourite with backpackers, run by an extrovert Gulf returner and his hospitable family. The rooms are huge and have long balconies overlooking coconut groves, two minutes' walk from the beach. Gabriel's cooking is famous too. **£**. **Golden Eye**, Gaura Waddo, tel: 227 7308; www.hotelgoldeneye.com. Situated on the sand; no pool, but the rooms are attractively done out and some have sea views. **££**. **Kerkar Retreat**, Gaura Waddo, tel: 2276017; www.subodhkerkar.com. Brainchild of a local artist, this is an upscale, 'boutique' guest house inspired by the colours, images and traditional architecture of Goa. **££**. **Pousada Tauma**, tel: 227 7535; www.pousada-tauma.com. More like a private mansion than a hotel, this bijou resort features laterite villas (designed by Dean D'Cruz) centred on a rambling pool with a swim-up bar and water cascade. The rooms are as stylish as you'd expect, and there's a small Ayurvedic spa and gourmet restaurant. **£££**

Candolim

Casa Sea Shell, Fort Aguada Rd, tel: 247 9879; email: seashellgoa@hotmail.com. Simple but large tiled rooms, all en-suite and with balconies, next to a well tended garden and secluded pool. Unbeatable value for money for this area. **£–££**. **Marbella**, Sinquerim, tel: 247 9551, email: marbella_goa@yahoo.com. One of Goa's most attractive hotels, shaded by giant mango trees. It's built in traditional Goan style, with azulejos, Indian antiques, blockprints and devotional sculpture adding a romantic feel to the suites. **££**. **Melodious Waves**, Sinquerim, tel: 247 9711; www.melodouswaves.com Modern, comfortable family guest house, with well furnished chalet-style rooms, close to the smartest strip of the beach. **££**. **Shanu's**, Escrivao Waddo, tel: 227 6899, email: shanu_goa@yahoo.com. This friendly mid-range place, whose comfortable rooms were recently re-vamped, has some of the only accommodation in Candolim actually on the beach. Great sunset views, but you pay more for the privilege. **£–££**. **Sonesta Inn**, Escrivao Waddo, tel: 222 7688; www.sonestainns.com. A smart package hotel, two minutes' walk from the sea, ranged around a large central pool. Most of the frills of a five-star, but on a smaller scale. **££**

Majorda/Utorda/Betalbatim

Kenilworth, Majorda, tel: 275 4180; www.kenilworthhotels.com. Swish five-star resort that recently had a major makeover and now boasts a state-of-the-art ayurvedic therapy suite and multi-gym. **£££**. **Park Hyatt**, Arossim Beach, tel: 272 1234; www.hyatt.com. Vast, ultra-luxurious five-star complex, comprising 251 rooms; some have their own "secret gardens" with outdoor showers. Pitched Mangalorean tiled roofs, wood beams and lathe-turned pillars give a "local" feel to the architecture, and the convoluted pool is reputedly the largest in India. **£££**. **Maneuelina**, Thond Waddo, Betalbatim, tel: 288 0154. One of the few budget guest houses in the area. The owner, beautician Sheryl Barretto, offers large, pleasant rooms, some with kitchenettes. **£**.

Morjim

Britto's Guest House, Vithaldas Waddo, tel: 224 4245. Scruffy but servicable rooms, commenable mainly for the zany, warm family atmosphere and location, in a traditional village on one of Goa's least exploited beaches. **£**. **Montego Bay**, Vithaldas Waddo, tel: 224 4222; www.montegobaygoa.com. Upmarket tourist camp, consisting of a dozen or so Rajasthani tents, stylishly fitted out and served by a good bar and restaurant. Right on the beach. **£££**.

Palolem-Patnem

Bhakti Kutir, Colomb, tel: 264 3469. A beautifully conceived "alternative resort" that uses local materials and styles, and sustainable technology, to create an environmentally friendly hotel. The rooms are all in magical "huts" with their own al-fresco showers and private, hidden terraces. **££**. **Cozy Nook**, north end of Palolem beach, tel: 264 3550. Nicest of the many Thai-style, huts-on-stilts places lining the palm groves, though correspondingly pricier. **£**. **Home**, Patnem, tel: 264 3916. Standard Goan-style rooms with pitched-tiled roofs and attached shower-toilets, upgraded by Swiss-British couple with floaty mosquito nets, bedside tables, lamps and other little touches to warrant the higher tariffs. **£**. **Oceanic**, Colomb, tel: 264 3059; www.hotel-oceanic.com. Very pleasant, British-run hotel on the outskirts of Palolem, boasting a pool and some of the most comfortable rooms in the area. A good

Miramar Beach

An auto in the Fontainhas quarter of Panaji

option if you want to be in this resort but aren't keen to rough it in a beach hut. **££**. **Sevas**, Colomb, tel: 09326 117674. Opposite Bhaki Kutir (see above), and very much in the same mould, although considerably cheaper. **££**. **Virgin Beach Resort**, Palolem, tel: 264 3451. Bright yellow and orange, three-storey block of smart rooms, very near the beach. **£**.

Panaji/Panjim

Panjim Inn/Panjim Pousada/Panjim People's, Fontainhas, tel: 2435628; www.panjiminn.com. Trio of small "heritage properties" in the heart of Panjim's old colonial quarter. Owner Ajit Sukhija is an antiques' buff, hence the lovely period furniture. The Pousada is pick of the bunch, with an atmospheric leafy balcony on the first floor. **££**. **Afonso Guest House**, Fontainhas, tel: 222 2359. Situated on a pretty Portuguese-style square, this spotlessly clean guest house is friendly and much the most appealing of the budget options in Panjim. **£**. **Goa Marriott**, Miramar Beach, tel: 243 7001; www.marriott.com. International hotel on the outskirts of town, facing the mouth of the river, with all the usual facilities you'd expect of a five-star. **£££**.

Rajbag

Goa InterContinental, Rajbag beach, tel: 264 4777, www.intercontinental.com. Ultra-luxurious resort (the most southerly and far-flung of the state's five-stars), with beach frontage, a topiary garden and nine-hole golf course. **£££**.

Siolim

Siolim House, Siolim, tel: 227 2138; www.siolimhouse.com. Grand Portuguese-era palacio converted with great taste and attention to period detail: four-posters, oyster-shell windows, mosaic floors and a big pool in the garden, and a gourmet restaurant. **££**.

Tirakol

Fort Tirakol, Tirakol, tel: 226 8258; www.nilayahermitage.com Newest of Goa's "heritage hotels", and the only one located inside an old fort; its ochre-washed ramparts overlook the estuary and a wonderful sandy beach. It successfully fuses old-world style with modern designer chic. **£££**.

Vagator

Bethany Inn, near China Garden restaurant, tel: 227 2731; www.bethanyinn.com. Well furnished self-contained doubles in a modern, efficient guest house at the top of the village, just off the main road. **£–££**. **Leoney Resort**, tel: 227 3634. this is the smartest option in Vagator: a group of mock Portuguese chalets, with polished wood doors and windows, laid out around a (kid-friendly) pool. The only catch is it's quite a walk (15 mins) from the beach. **££**.

Vainguinim

Cidade de Goa, Vainguinim beach, tel: 222 1133; www.cidadedegoa.com. Designed by Arundhati Roy's former husband, Charles Correa, and one of Goa's top five-star deluxe hotels, spread in pastel-coloured boxes behind a quiet little cove. Convenient for Panaji. **£££**.

Varca/Cavelossim/Mobor

Dona Sa Maria, Cavelossim, tel: 274 5290; www.donasamaria.com. Impeccably kept family-run hotel, formerly a package place but now independent, with its own small pool. Peaceful Tamborim beach lies 15 minutes' walk across the paddy fields. **££**. **Dona Sylvia**, Mobor, tel: 287 1321, www.donasylvia.com. Lively, modern complex with 176 rooms specialising in all-inclusive packages. Good watersports facilities and direct access to the beach. **£££**. **The Leela**, Cavelossim, tel: 287 1234; www.ghmhotels.com. Luxury hotels don't come much more luxurious than this (although it's lost its 'Grandest Place to Stay in Goa' crown to the newer Park-Hyatt at Arossim (see p.93) in recent years). A casino and nightclub (Acqui) make it popular with staggeringly wealthy Russians. **£££**. **Ramada-Caravela Beach Resort**, Varca Beach, tel: 274 5200; www.ramada.com. Sprawling five-star resort whose Goa-themed decor, disco, and open-air pool area verge on kitsch, but have been pulling in package tourists and rich honeymooners from Bangalore for over a decade. **£££**.

Excursions

Gokarna

Nimmu's, behind the beach, tel: 0838/656730. Large budget guest house, and the only foreigner-oriented place to stay in town. The rooms are clean and have bathrooms. Only a stone's throw away from the temples and town beach, but a peaceful location nonetheless. **£**. **Hotel Gokarna International**, Kumta Taluk, Gokarna, tel: 0838 657368/656848. A more comfortable option than Nimmu's, and very good value for money, though on the main road at the entrance to the town and thus prone to traffic noise in the day. **£**.

Hampi

Shanti Lodge, behind Virupaksha temple, tel: 0839 441568. Very basic, but acceptably clean guest house with shared showers and toilets, opening on to a leafy central courtyard. The rooms are a bit dingy, but there's relaxing roofspace. If it's full, Rahul (tel: 0839 411648), south of the main bazaar, is the best fallback. **£**.

Hospet

Malligi Tourist Home, 6/143 Jambunatha Rd, tel: 0839 428101. Well managed and comfortable hotel offering a range of differently priced rooms. Amenities include a large pool, billiards' room and massage centre. **£–££**. **Priyadarshini**, MG Rd, tel: 0839 428838. Not quite as appealing as the Malligi, but spotless and secure. It also has a couple of good restaurants. **£–££**.

Fruit for sale

Index

© APA Publications GmbH & Co. Verlag KG Singapore Branch, Singapore.

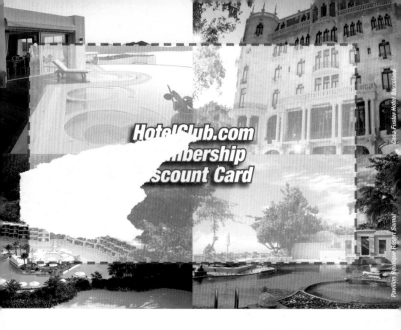

Casa Fuster Hotel Barcelona

Pavilion Boutique Resort Samui

Register with

HotelClub.com
and get **£10!**

At *HotelClub.com*, we reward our Members with discounts and free stays in their favourite hotels. As a Member, every booking made by you through *HotelClub.com* will earn you Member Dollars.

When you register, we will credit your account with *£10* which you can use for your next booking! The equivalent of *£10* will be credited in US$ to your Member account (as *HotelClub Member Dollars*). All you need to do is log on to *www.HotelClub.com/compactguides*. Complete your details, including the Membership Number and Password located on the back of the *HotelClub.com* card.

Over 2.2 million Members already use Member Dollars to pay for all or part of their hotel bookings. Join now and start spending Member Dollars whenever and wherever you want – you are not restricted to specific hotels or dates!

With great savings of up to 60% on over 20,000 hotels across 97 countries, you are sure to find the perfect location for business or pleasure.
Happy travels from *HotelClub.com!*

INSIGHT GUIDES
www.insightguides.com

 HotelClub.com

OVER 250 DESTINATIONS
IN 14 LANGUAGES

Let us be your guide

Your first visit – or a familiar destination? A short stay – or an extended exploration? Whatever your needs, there's an Insight Guide in a format to suit you. From Alaska to Zanzibar, we'll help you discover your world with great pictures, insightful text, easy-to-use maps, and invaluable advice.

www.insightguides.com